Dashing Dish

100 Simple and Delicious Recipes for Clean Eating

KATIE FARRELL

WITHDRAWN

NELSON
BOOKS

An Imprint of Thomas Nelson

© 2014 by Katie Elise Farrell

Published in Nashville, Tennessee, by Nelson Books, an imprint of Thomas Nelson. Nelson Books and Thomas Nelson are registered trademarks of HarperCollins Christian Publishing, Inc.

Thomas Nelson titles may be purchased in bulk for educational, business, fund-raising, or sales promotional use. For information, please e-mail SpecialMarkets@ThomasNelson.com.

Library of Congress Control Number: 2014945328

ISBN-13: 978-0-7180-2161-0

Printed in the United States of America

14 15 16 17 18 QGF 6 5 4 3 2 1

CONTENTS

INTRODUCTION

The *Dashing Dish Cookbook* is filled with one hundred healthy recipes that let you eat some of your most craved comfort foods in a healthy way. Every delicious recipe is simple to make, with a focus on clean eating. The philosophy behind this cookbook is that healthy eating should be flavorful and easy. I hope this cookbook brings a fresh perspective on living a healthy lifestyle, as well as a sense of joy as you whip up each recipe!

IN *THE DASHING DISH COOKBOOK* YOU WILL FIND:

100 healthy and wholesome recipes. Staying true to the Dashing Dish website, every recipe in this cookbook is made with healthy, wholesome ingredients. A pantry staple list is included that will help you stock up on all of the basic ingredients you will need to make these dishes.

Nutrition information. Every recipe lists the calorie, fiber, carbohydrate, sugar, fat, and protein content for each serving. This will help keep you and your family informed and knowledgeable about nutrition and portion control. It is important to note that the nutrition information provided is based on the specific ingredients used to develop the recipes; therefore, there may be nutritional variation on the ingredients used. The nutrition is calculated based on the primary ingredients listed. The stated calculations do not include the substitutions, optional ingredients, or the additional ingredients suggested for serving.

Simple and kid-friendly recipes. All of the recipes in this book are uncomplicated and made with a few basic ingredients, just like the recipes you know and love from the Dashing Dish website. Many are picky-eater friendly and can be made by both experienced and novice chefs alike!

Tips and tricks. Along with the recipes in this cookbook, I have also included healthy baking and cooking techniques that will help save you time and money.

There are few things that bring me greater joy than cooking healthy food and teaching others how fun and simple it can be to live a healthy lifestyle, and I hope to bring that same passion to you!

CLEAN EATING TIPS

The term *clean eating* has become quite popular these days, yet many people are not exactly sure what the phrase means. Clean eating is not a diet; it's a lifestyle approach to eating. This way of eating incorporates whole foods that have not been altered or processed, and that have no chemicals and harmful preservatives added.

Most *Dashing Dish* recipes in this book and on my website are conducive with the clean-eating lifestyle because they call for ingredients in their most natural states and include few, if any, processed ingredients. *Dashing Dish* baked goods are a good example, as they are prepared using whole grain oats rather than white or whole wheat flours, which are essentially whole grains that have been stripped of their nutrients.

There are many benefits to eating clean. Some of the most common are weight loss, increased energy, and improved digestion. Here are a few basic choices from each food group that are considered to be clean eating:

PROTEIN SOURCES: chicken, turkey, fish, egg whites, Greek yogurt, cottage cheese, protein powder

VEGETABLES: broccoli, cauliflower, zucchini, squash, green beans, onions, sweet potatoes

FRUIT: strawberries, apples, blueberries, bananas

WHOLE GRAIN SOURCES: old-fashioned oats, high-fiber pasta, high-fiber wrap bread, Ezekiel or whole grain bread

FAT SOURCES: avocados, nuts, nut butters

SWEETENERS: stevia, honey, agave nectar, maple syrup

SHOULD I COUNT CALORIES?

I have received many questions on the blog about counting calories, so I thought I would share my perspective on what has worked well in my own life. In general, I believe that counting calories can be beneficial for someone who is just starting to read nutrition labels and become familiar with different foods. However, I always suggest that our ultimate goal should be to listen to our bodies rather than counting calories.

In the beginning stages of a weight-loss journey, counting calories can be helpful. It can provide a realistic sense of how to space out calories throughout the day, as well as help learn proper portion sizes. But when it comes to maintaining this long term, counting calories isn't very realistic, and at times it can become obsessive if taken to the extreme.

I found that counting calories for about a month in the beginning of my journey worked well for me because it taught me how to spread out my meals in a way that made me feel energized throughout the day. After learning proper portion sizes, I decided to stop tracking calories and start listening to my body's natural hunger cues. I also learned how to listen to my body and know when I was full to avoid overeating.

I still continue to pay attention to the number of calories, fat, sugar, fiber, carbohydrates, and protein in food. However, this is more about being informed and aware of what I am putting into my body. Although I am conscious of what I am eating, I do not keep a running total of calories for the day. Here are a few reasons why I do not count calories:

1. **Eating with friends and family can get tricky if you are always counting calories.** In general, if you don't know what was put in the food, there is no way to accurately count the calories and this can lead to anxiety. Instead, when I am at a gathering, I try to pick the healthiest choices that I see and make it my goal to focus more on enjoying the people I'm with than on the food. After all, that is what life is all about, isn't it? If I do pick a dessert or something that I know isn't extremely healthy, then I stick to one portion and spend time enjoying each bite.

2. **If you count calories, you may overeat.** Here's what I mean: If you count calories, then chances are you will feel like you need to finish every single bite, even if you are truly full, in an effort to track the calories properly. This is a bit crazy if you think about it, because God put a full signal inside each one of us for a reason. When I was first learning to pay attention to my body, I would take a few bites, put my fork down, and be aware of how I felt. Then, when I was satisfied, I stopped eating and saved the rest for later. Sure, it was tough to do this at first, and it does take practice (and prayer) in the beginning, but eventually you will be so in tune with your body that you won't even have to think about it!

3. **It can lead to bingeing.** For me personally, counting calories led to binges when I let myself have a day off from counting. On the days that I wasn't counting calories, I felt as though I had to eat everything like it was my last chance to eat, knowing that the next day I was going to be back to tracking everything I put into my mouth. In those moments, I felt like I had to revel in my freedom by eating whatever came across my path.

Those are just a few of the reasons I don't advocate counting calories long term. On that note, I will say that everyone is different, and everyone has different things that work for them. Find what works for you to help keep you on track and keep your body healthy.

Try counting calories for about a month so that you can get an idea of how much to eat and become familiar with composing meals that are well balanced. When the foundation is established, you should be able to move into listening to your body and eating until you are satisfied. This is how God created our bodies to function! He gave us the ability to know when we are hungry and when we are full so that we would eat only what our bodies truly need. Also, with this approach I find it is easier to put the focus on eating healthy and nutritious foods rather than on the numbers.

When this principle is combined with the main principles of healthy eating (limiting the amount of processed foods and sugar, having a good balance of protein and fiber with meals, and eating nutritious snacks in between meals), you should be able to maintain a healthy weight in a way that is sustainable for life!

DASHING DISH STAPLES

One of my primary goals with *Dashing Dish* recipes is to keep the recipes simple, quick, and made with a few basic ingredients that most people have in their kitchens while being delicious and using "clean" (not processed) ingredients. With these ingredients on hand, you'll be able to make almost any recipe in *Dashing Dish*.

PROTEIN AND MEATS

Lean pork tenderloin
Extra-lean ground turkey or beef
Boneless, skinless chicken breasts
Salmon and tilapia
Beans (garbanzo, black, kidney, and white)
Protein powder (such as Vanilla Designer Whey)

DAIRY

Low-fat cottage cheese
Plain low-fat or nonfat Greek yogurt

Unsweetened almond milk (or low-fat milk)
Cheese (grated Parmesan, thin-sliced or shredded reduced-fat Cheddar, feta, thin-sliced Swiss)
Eggs and egg whites

BREADS, GRAINS, AND FLOURS

Ezekiel bread and whole grain bread
High-fiber wrap bread (such as La Tortilla)
Quinoa and whole grain rice

Old-fashioned oats (use gluten-
  free if sensitive)
Oat flour (made from old-
  fashioned oats ground in a
  blender or food processor)
Almonds and almond flour
  (made from almonds ground in
  a blender or food processor)
Peanut flour

VEGETABLES

Year-Round
Broccoli
Onions
Spinach
Cauliflower
Sweet potatoes
Lettuce
Bell peppers
Corn

Spring and Summer
Zucchini
Summer squash

Fall and Winter
Spaghetti squash
Butternut squash
Pumpkin

Fruit
Tomatoes

Berries
Avocados
Bananas
Apples
Unsweetened applesauce

*Seasonings, Condiments, and
Other*
Salt and black pepper
Onion powder and dried minced
  onion
Minced garlic and garlic powder
Italian seasoning (or basil and
  oregano mixture)
Ground cinnamon
Parsley
Chili powder
Taco seasoning (or cumin, chili
  seasoning, and salt)
Pumpkin and apple pie spice
Stevia (baking or packets)
Unsweetened cocoa powder
Honey and low-sugar maple syrup
Hummus
Low-sugar ketchup
Prepared mustard
White vinegar, rice vinegar, and
  red wine vinegar
Natural whipped topping (such
  as truwhip)
Cooking spray

DASHING DISH TIPS

Here are a few simple tips for making *Dashing Dish* recipes with ease!

- Use foil or silicone muffin liners when preparing muffins or baked goods and spray with cooking spray. The muffins pop out of the liners without sticking. I do not recommend using paper liners because the batter tends to stick to them.
- Refrigerate *Dashing Dish* baked goods. Unlike store-bought baked goods, they do not contain preservatives and will spoil quickly without refrigeration. Most homemade baked goods last 5 to 7 days in the fridge. You can also freeze them for up to 3 months.
- Make oat and almond flour in big batches. I like to pour a large container of oats or a bag of almonds into the blender or food processor and blend into a flour. Then pour the flour in a sealed container and freeze for up to one year.
- Converting old-fashioned oats to oat flour in recipes is simple. When the recipe calls for old-fashioned oats, but you have oat flour on hand, simply use $1/4$ cup less oat flour than the old-fashioned oats that the recipe calls for (example: a recipe calls for 1 cup old-fashioned oats; use $3/4$ cup oat flour).
- If you are gluten sensitive, be sure to use gluten-free products. When using old-fashioned oats, be sure they are gluten-free oats.
- When a recipe calls for cooked chicken, I like to use the white meat from a rotisserie chicken or make my own shredded chicken in large batches in a slow cooker and store the meat in the freezer. It helps to always have cooked chicken on hand to add to recipes.

TOP TEN TIPS FOR EATING HEALTHY ON A BUDGET

Eating healthy does not have to mean expensive grocery bills. Here are some of my favorite tips for eating healthy on a budget.

Plan ahead. Make a grocery list and stick to it. The best way to avoid impulse buying is to write down what you are going to buy before you get to the store so you won't be tempted to get things you don't need.

Be prepared. Pack lunches and snacks, and eat before you go out. When you pack your own food, you prevent yourself from overeating, you always know what is in your food, and you save time and money.

Buy in bulk. There are times when it's smart to buy in bulk. For example, buy discounted meat in big batches and store it in your freezer until you are ready to use it. It's also smart to buy products in bulk that you use a lot. Compare smaller quantities with the bigger version; often it is cheaper to buy the larger quantity if you are going to use it all.

Buy frozen. If you think you won't be able to use something up before it spoils, such as fruit or vegetables, buy them frozen. Not only will this save you money but it will prevent you from throwing money away on spoiled groceries.

Buy in-season produce. Food grown in season is not only more affordable, it also tastes better. Look for root vegetables in the winter; apples, potatoes, and squash in the fall; and broccoli and berries in the summer. Farmers' markets may also have a better deal on produce than grocery stores.

Buy generic. Name brands often have increased prices due to the packaging and advertising costs.

Clip coupons. Sign up for newsletters about sales and deals at the stores where you frequently shop. Investing a few minutes clipping or printing coupons each week can save you a lot of money on groceries.

Get the customer card. Many grocery stores hold sales and specials for customer card holders only. Signing up for these costumer cards is often free and only takes a few moments.

Buy a water bottle. Don't spend money on soft drinks, juices, or bottled water. Instead, invest in a few nice water bottles and refill them. Not only will this save you money but it will save you tons of sugar and calories!

Get creative with leftovers. If you happen to have leftovers of some of your ingredients, don't throw them away. Instead, put them to good use and get creative with different recipes, or freeze them if possible.

DASHING DISH'S EATING OUT GUIDE

Be prepared. If possible, go online before going to a restaurant to see what options sound good to you that are reasonably healthy. A lot of restaurants offer nutrition information online now, and if not, the calories for specific dishes can often be found using search engines. Try looking for something with around 500 calories or less (unless you plan on splitting an entrée with someone).

Watch portions. Most restaurant portions are double what a normal portion size should be. Eat slowly and pay attention to when you are truly satisfied (not stuffed), and get a to-go box to take the leftovers home. Another great way to portion control is to split an entrée with someone.

Beware of salad dressings. If you order a salad, always ask for low-fat dressing on the side. If low-fat dressing is not an option, dip your fork in the dressing before each bite.

Look carefully at salad toppings. When choosing a salad, make sure none of the ingredients are fried (if they are, ask to have them left off). Also, ask for high-fat ingredients (such as nuts and cheeses) to be put on the side so you can control how much goes on.

Skip the bread basket. The bread served before meals is truly nothing but empty calories, and generally a lot of empty calories. With butter, it could easily add up to 500 calories, which is the calorie content of an entire meal!

Don't drink your calories. Stick with water or sparkling water. If you must have alcohol, limit yourself to one drink. A glass of wine, a light beer, or a shot of hard liquor mixed with club soda all have around 100 calories (which is much better than mixed drinks, which can contain hundreds of calories for one drink!).

Know your terms. As a general rule, order foods that are broiled, grilled, roasted, or steamed. Steer clear of foods that are fried, sautéed, or blackened, which means they are cooked in a pan with oil.

Don't be embarrassed to make special requests. With all of the allergies out there today, you can be sure that waitstaff and cooks are very used to getting special orders. If you ask for no butter, sauce on the side, or steamed versus sautéed, you could save yourself hundreds of calories that you will never even miss!

TIPS FOR DEVELOPING HEALTHY HABITS

Living a healthy lifestyle does not have to be hard work or a drastic change. The best place to start is by making small changes in your everyday life. Making simple swaps and setting small goals will add up over time, and before you know it, these changes will become habits.

Here are some simple changes that will have a huge effect:

INSTEAD OF:

▶ White sugar
▶ White flour
▶ White pasta
▶ Butter (or any unhealthy fats, such as fried foods)
▶ Processed snacks (such as crackers, chips, cookies, etc.)

TRY:

▶ Stevia, honey (or natural sweetener of choice other than white sugar)
▶ Oat flour (or if you're feeling really adventurous, try almond or coconut flour)
▶ High-fiber pasta or quinoa

- Unsweetened applesauce
- Plain low-fat or nonfat Greek yogurt
- Olive oil (in moderation)
- Snacks with whole grains and no added sugar (such as *Dashing Dish* muffins)

The key to setting goals is making sure they are attainable and realistic. Here are some examples of short-term goals to get you started:

* Aim to eat three small meals with two to three snacks in between. This will keep your metabolism fueled and your blood sugar levels stabilized.
* Eat every three to four hours. This will also help stabilize blood sugar levels.
* Drink more water, and replace any other beverages you are currently drinking with water. Add lemon or lime juice for flavor if you desire.
* Get moving! Aim to be active for at least thirty to sixty minutes per day. This could be going to the gym, walking, cleaning, playing with your kids, or dancing around your house.

HEALTHY SNACKS

There is something about a snack that gives us the energy boost we often need to make it through the day. Snacks are great because they usually don't require a lot of thought or preparation, and yet they can be delicious and satisfying. I generally eat one or two snacks each day, and they are usually between 100 and 200 calories each. I try to incorporate some protein and fiber into my snacks to keep me satisfied until my next meal. Here are some of my favorite snack ideas.

ON-THE-GO SNACKS

▸ Low-fat or nonfat Greek yogurt: I like buying the plain or vanilla flavors and adding stevia or honey and frozen fruit.
▸ Protein bars: I like ones that have less than 200 calories, more than 10 grams of protein, and less than 10 grams of sugar.
▸ *Dashing Dish* muffins
▸ Apples
▸ Cheese sticks
▸ 100-calorie packs of almonds

AT-HOME SNACKS

▸ 100-calorie popcorn
▸ *Dashing Dish* protein shakes or smoothies

- Sweet potatoes: microwaved or baked
- *Dashing Dish* single-serve muffins and cakes
- Greek yogurt parfaits: nonfat Greek yogurt layered with fruit, nuts, peanut butter, oatmeal, or *Dashing Dish* granola
- Egg white omelet with vegetables
- Fresh vegetables with hummus
- Frozen fruit

MEAL PLANNING

Does the thought of preparing food for your family during the week overwhelm you or seem like just one more thing on your to-do list? Preparing three meals a day is not always easy, but it can be done! I have found that the best way to live a healthy lifestyle and have healthy and delicious meals all week long is much easier when you plan your meals ahead of time.

There are so many benefits to meal planning. Meal planning will save you time and money and will help you eat healthy. Here are a few simple steps to help you plan and prepare your meals in a short time for the week.

STEP 1: PLAN AND SHOP

The first step to meal planning is writing out the meals and snacks you would like to eat for the week. This can be done on a calendar or as a list. Next, look over the ingredients for each recipe and make a grocery list based on the items you will need. Then it's off to the grocery store!

STEP 2: PREPARE THE FOOD

When you get home from the grocery store, take everything out of the grocery bags and set the items out on the counter. Organize the ingredients according to each recipe. It's time to get cooking!

STEP 3: PUT EVERYTHING TOGETHER
TO MAKE THE RECIPES

Many of the *Dashing Dish* breakfast recipes are quick and easy to make so you don't necessarily need to prepare your breakfasts ahead of time, but it never hurts to plan ahead. You can make something such as protein muffins for the week and pack them in a zip-top bag for busy mornings.

Lunches can easily be made ahead of time and put together in an assembly-line fashion. If you're making salads or sandwiches, you can prepare for the entire week by making them all at once in Tupperware containers or by wrapping them individually in foil. You can also make a big batch of soup or chili and divide it into portions for the week.

Dinners can be put together ahead of time and baked just before you eat. This way your meals are always warm and fresh. You can also cook your meat and chop your vegetables at the beginning of the week so they are ready when you need them.

STEP 4: PUT IT ALL AWAY!

After all the food is prepped and the recipes are made, put everything in sealed containers and place the containers in the fridge so you'll have something to grab if you are heading out for the day or to quickly heat up for a delicious meal in minutes.

If you plan ahead you will see how easy it can be to prepare meals for the week in just one day. Soon meal planning will become a part of your routine and will save you time, money, and stress!

STAYING HEALTHY DURING SPECIAL OCCASIONS

Special occasions are generally filled with family, friends, and food. Here are a few tips to help you enjoy the holidays in a balanced way!

1. Choose a healthy alternative. Eating healthy year-round, even during special occasions and the holidays, can be done. Eating healthy does not mean you have to give up the foods you enjoy most. There are simple swaps you can make with healthier alternatives. *Dashing Dish* recipes help you swap out ingredients while still keeping your mind and stomach satisfied.

2. Pick and choose your treats. Special occasions are often celebrated with food and treats. There is nothing wrong with enjoying some of your favorite foods, but do it in moderation. Choose what you want to splurge on and savor every bite!

3. Be prepared. One way to prevent overeating is by eating small, frequent meals throughout the day and having a protein snack before heading off to parties or celebrations. When you sit down to eat a meal, you will be able to properly pay attention to your body's hunger cues because you won't be overly famished to begin with.

4. The party is about more than what is on your plate. Food is an element of a celebration, but not the defining factor or the most important part. If you keep this in mind when you're on your way to

a party, you can remind yourself that spending time with family and friends is the highlight of the event. This helps take the focus off the food and puts it back on the things that matter most.

5. It's okay to say no. During special occasions and holidays, many people are giving treats away as gifts or offering food as a gesture of love. It is okay to be honest and politely say, "No, thank you." Most people will respect you when you graciously say no. This allows you to say yes to the things you truly do enjoy!

6. Bring your own dish to pass. If you bring your own dish to pass, you can offer something that is tasty and healthy! *The Dashing Dish Cookbook* is filled with options that are great to bring to a celebration or get-together. These recipes are just as rich and delicious as the traditional dishes, so no one will even know it is healthy until you tell them!

7. Learn to bounce back. I find that one of the greatest downfalls when it comes to overeating during a special occasion is that it sets most people on a dangerous slippery slope. If you do overeat or make bad choices, don't make the mistake of giving up or feeling guilty. Remember, it is not one meal that will make you unhealthy, so don't let it get you in a defeated mind-set! Just make the simple choice to bounce back. Start the next day by being active and get right back on track with a healthy lifestyle.

SWEETENER CONVERSIONS

You will notice that the ingredients call for a sweetener that measures like sugar, which includes any sweetener that can be measured the same as sugar, or you could use sugar if you prefer. However, please note that using sugar will alter the nutritional information provided.

If you prefer to use sugar, stevia packets, baking stevia blend, stevia liquid, or stevia powder, you will have to alter the amount based on the conversion table on the next page, or according to your desired taste. This can take some experimenting, but once you get a feel for baking with different types of sweeteners, it is very simple to know how much to use. To get you started, I have provided a simple conversion table that works with stevia.

Please also note that the amounts listed below may vary based on the brand of stevia you are using. The following chart pertains to NuNaturals Stevia, which is the brand I recommend.

Sugar	Stevia Packets	Baking Stevia Blend	Stevia Liquid	Stevia Powder
2 teaspoons	1 packet	1 teaspoon	1/4 teaspoon	1/2 teaspoon
1/4 cup	6 packets	2 tablespoons	1 1/2 teaspoons	1 tablespoon
1/2 cup	12 packets	4 tablespoons	2 teaspoons	2 tablespoons
3/4 cup	18 packets	6 tablespoons	4 1/2 teaspoons	3 tablespoons
1 cup	24 packets	1/2 cup	2 tablespoons	4 tablespoons
2 cups	48 packets	1 cup	4 tablespoons	8 tablespoons

BREAKFAST

NO-BAKE COOKIE PANCAKES

Estimated Time: 15 minutes

1 ripe medium banana

4 large egg whites

2 tablespoons unsweetened almond milk (or low-fat milk)

1 tablespoon peanut butter

1/2 teaspoon butter extract (or vanilla extract)

1/2 cup old-fashioned oats

1/4 cup protein powder

2 teaspoons unsweetened cocoa powder

2 tablespoons sweetener that measures like sugar

1 teaspoon baking powder

1/8 teaspoon salt

1 tablespoon mini chocolate chips

Heat a nonstick griddle or large nonstick pan coated with cooking spray over medium heat. In a small bowl mash the banana and add the egg whites, almond milk, peanut butter, and butter extract and mix. In a medium bowl mix together the oats, protein powder, cocoa powder, sweetener, baking powder, and salt. Add the banana mixture into the oat mixture and mix until the batter is smooth and well combined. Pour 1/4 cup batter for each pancake onto the heated griddle or nonstick pan. Sprinkle a few chocolate chips on each pancake before flipping. When the pancakes bubble, flip and cook until the other side is golden brown.

Yields 2 Servings
Nutritional Information Per Serving: 306 calories; 9 grams fat; 36 grams carbohydrates; 6 grams fiber; 9 grams sugar; 27 grams protein

When I was a kid I made no-bake chocolate peanut butter cookies all of the time and have loved them ever since. One day I had a novel idea. Why not make them into pancakes? Now I can enjoy one of my favorite cookies for breakfast, but in the form of a protein-packed pancake!

CAKE BATTER PROTEIN SHAKE

🕐 Estimated Time: 5 minutes

One of my favorite ice-cream flavors is cake batter. This protein shake is a rich and creamy spin on my favorite ice cream that is healthy enough to eat for breakfast! Have a "party" for breakfast with this Cake Batter Protein Shake!

1/2 cup low-fat cottage cheese

1/4 cup vanilla or plain protein powder

1/2 teaspoon almond extract

2 tablespoons sweetener that measures like sugar, or to taste

1/2 to 1 cup water (alter this according to desired consistency)

5 to 10 ice cubes (use fewer for a thinner consistency)

Add the cottage cheese, protein powder, almond extract, sweetener, water, and ice cubes to a blender and blend until a creamy consistency is reached.

Yields 1 Serving
Nutritional Information: 187 calories; 2 grams fat; 5 grams carbohydrates; 0 grams fiber; 3 grams sugar; 35 grams protein

CARROT CAKE PANCAKES

🕐 Estimated Time: 15 to 20 minutes

Pancakes

1/4 cup vanilla or plain protein powder

1/2 cup plain nonfat Greek yogurt (or plain low-fat yogurt)

1 cup old-fashioned oats

2 large egg whites

3/4 cup grated carrots, divided

1/2 teaspoon ground cinnamon

Pinch of ground ginger

Pinch of ground nutmeg

Pinch of salt

1/2 teaspoon baking powder

1 to 2 tablespoons sweetener that measures like sugar

1/2 cup water

2 tablespoons chopped walnuts, optional

2 tablespoons golden raisins, optional

Optional Cream–Cheese Frosting

1/2 cup (4-ounce) low-fat cream cheese, softened

1/4 cup low-sugar or low-sugar maple syrup

1/2 to 1 tablespoon sweetener that measures like sugar

Dash of ground cinnamon

Carrot cake is one of the wonderful delicacies in life. Moist, rich cake slathered with a creamy cream cheese frosting . . . now that is my kind of dessert! So, in honor of my love for carrot cake, I decided to re-create this ever-popular cake into something that is excusable to eat for breakfast. You can certainly top these "cakes" with maple syrup, but why not use cream cheese frosting? If you enjoy carrot cake and pancakes, then you will love this protein-packed combination.

To make the pancakes: Heat a nonstick griddle or a large nonstick skillet coated with cooking spray over medium heat. In a blender add the protein powder, yogurt, oats, egg whites, 1/2 cup grated carrots, cinnamon, ginger, nutmeg, salt, baking powder, and sweetener and blend until smooth. Stir in the additional 1/4 cup grated carrots, and walnuts and raisins if desired. Spoon about 1/4 cup of batter per pancake onto the griddle or skillet. Turn when the pancakes bubble and the edges are cooked.

To make the cream cheese frosting: In a small bowl whisk together the cream cheese, syrup, sweetener, and cinnamon until smooth. Drizzle over pancakes if desired and enjoy!

Yields 3 Servings
Nutritional Information Per Serving: 175 calories; 2 grams fat; 22 grams carbohydrates; 3 grams fiber; 3 grams sugar; 18 grams protein

PROTEIN-PACKED BANANA BREAD OATMEAL

🕐 Estimated Time: 5 minutes

What could be better than enjoying a bowl of warm and filling oatmeal that tastes like banana bread and is packed with protein? This oatmeal makes an excellent breakfast or snack and is so delicious you'll have a hard time believing that it is actually good for you!

1/2 cup old-fashioned oats

1 cup unsweetened almond milk (or low-fat milk)

1/2 large banana (fresh or frozen and thawed), mashed

2 to 4 teaspoons sweetener that measures like sugar

1/2 teaspoon vanilla extract

Dash of ground cinnamon

Pinch of ground nutmeg

Pinch of salt

2 large egg whites, well beaten

2 tablespoons protein powder, optional

1 tablespoon chopped walnuts or pecans, optional

Pour the oats into a microwave-safe bowl and add almond milk (or milk). Microwave for 2 to 2 1/2 minutes and remove from the microwave. Stir in the mashed banana, sweetener, vanilla, cinnamon, nutmeg, salt, and egg whites. Whisk until everything is well combined. Microwave an additional 2 to 3 minutes, or until desired consistency is reached. Stir in the protein powder if desired. Top with nuts if desired.

Yields 1 Serving
Nutritional Information: 286 calories; 7 grams fat; 45 grams carbohydrates; 7 grams fiber; 10 grams sugar; 14 grams protein

THE BEST GIANT FRITTATA

○ Estimated Time: 45 minutes

Frittata

1 medium zucchini or summer squash, cut in half lengthwise and diced into bite-size pieces

2 cups frozen cauliflower (or 2 cups fresh, chopped into bite-size pieces)

2 cups frozen broccoli florets (or 2 cups fresh, chopped into bite-size pieces)

1 small onion, finely chopped

1 medium bell pepper (color of choice), diced into bite-size pieces

1 cup frozen chopped spinach, thawed and squeezed dry (or 2 cups fresh)

1 cup water (or more depending on cooking)

12 large egg whites (or 2 cups liquid egg whites)

2 large eggs (or an additional 1/2 cup liquid egg whites)

1/2 teaspoon salt

1/4 teaspoon black pepper

1/4 cup grated Parmesan cheese

Toppings

1/2 cup mozzarella cheese

2 tablespoons grated Parmesan cheese

2 Roma tomatoes (or 1 large tomato), sliced into disks

4 to 8 slices ham or turkey lunchmeat, chopped into bite-size pieces, optional

2 to 3 pieces center-cut bacon, cooked and crumbled, optional

A frittata is essentially a giant omelet made in a skillet. The best part about a frittata is the ease of making it. You don't have to go through the hassle of flipping the eggs as you would with an omelet. This giant frittata can be made for breakfast, lunch, or dinner on any day of the week.

Preheat the oven to 450 degrees. Spray a very large oven-safe nonstick skillet with cooking spray. Add the zucchini, cauliflower, broccoli, onions, bell peppers, and spinach to the skillet along with 1 cup water (you may need more if you are using fresh veggies rather than frozen). Place the skillet over medium-high heat and cover. Cook the vegetables 3 to 5 minutes, or until they are tender, stirring occasionally. When the vegetables are tender remove the lid and continue to cook until all of the water has evaporated. (Note: You may have to add about 1/2 cup water if vegetables are not done cooking at this point but the water has dried up. This will keep the veggies from burning in the pan.)

When the vegetables are tender and the water has evaporated, turn off the heat and pour the vegetables into a medium bowl. In a large bowl whisk together the egg whites, eggs, salt, pepper, and Parmesan cheese. Add the vegetable mixture to the eggs slowly, one spoonful at a time, to keep the vegetables from cooking the eggs.

Clean out the skillet used to cook the vegetables and re-spray with cooking spray. Add the egg mixture back to the pan or pour into a 9 x 13-inch baking dish. Top with mozzarella, Parmesan, sliced tomatoes, and ham and bacon if desired.

Bake in preheated oven for 35 to 45 minutes or until the frittata is cooked through and slightly golden brown on the top. Cut into 8 equal servings.

Yields 8 Servings
Nutritional Information Per Serving: 113 calories; 4 grams fat; 7.5 grams carbohydrates; 3 grams fiber; 0 grams sugar; 15 grams protein

PEANUT BUTTER BREAKFAST BARS

The morning can be one of the busiest times of the day, yet it is also the most important time to have a well-balanced meal. It is always shocking when people tell me they don't eat breakfast. More often than not, it is because they simply don't have time in the morning. These breakfast bars are extremely simple to make, and they are so incredibly delicious that you will feel like you are eating dessert for breakfast!

1/2 cup peanut butter

1/2 cup mashed banana

1/2 cup unsweetened almond milk (or low-fat milk)

2 large egg whites

1 cup old-fashioned oats

1/4 teaspoon baking soda

1/2 teaspoon baking powder

1/4 teaspoon salt

1/2 cup sweetener that measures like sugar

1/2 cup vanilla protein powder (or flavor of choice)

Preheat the oven to 350 degrees. Spray a 9 x 9-inch baking pan with cooking spray. Soften peanut butter in the microwave for 30 seconds in a small microwave-safe bowl. In a large bowl mix together the softened peanut butter with the banana, almond milk, egg whites, oats, baking soda, baking powder, salt, sweetener, and protein powder until everything is well combined. Pour the batter into the prepared baking pan. Bake for 15 to 20 minutes or until a toothpick inserted in the center comes out clean. Remove from the oven and let cool completely. Cut into 8 equal bars. Wrap each bar in plastic wrap or foil and store in the refrigerator (for up to 7 days) or freezer (for up to one month) for a quick and healthy breakfast or snack.

Yields 8 Servings
Nutritional Information Per Serving: 177 calories; 9 grams fat; 13 grams carbohydrates; 2.5 grams fiber; 2 grams sugar; 13 grams protein

NOTE: If you don't have protein powder you can use an additional 1/2 cup oats.

BLUEBERRY PANCAKE MUFFINS

🕐 Estimated Time: 25 minutes

1 1/2 cups oats

1/2 cup unsweetened applesauce

1/4 cup low-sugar maple syrup

1/4 cup skim milk (or low-fat milk)

2 large egg whites

1 teaspoon maple (or vanilla) extract

1/2 cup sweetener that measures like sugar

1 teaspoon baking powder

1/8 teaspoon baking soda

1/4 teaspoon salt

1 cup fresh blueberries, divided (or 1/2 cup frozen blueberries, thawed and drained of juice)

Preheat the oven to 350 degrees. Line a 12-cup muffin tin with foil or silicone liners and spray with cooking spray. Combine the oats, applesauce, syrup, milk, egg whites, maple extract, sweetener, baking powder, baking soda, and salt in a blender. Blend until the mixture is smooth. Pour the mixture into a medium bowl and gently fold in 3/4 cup blueberries. Spoon the batter into 12 muffin cups, filling each cup almost full. Bake for 18 to 20 minutes or until a toothpick inserted in the center of a muffin comes out clean. Halfway through baking add the additional 1/4 cup blueberries to the muffins. Remove the muffins from the pan immediately and allow to cool at room temperature on a cooling rack.

Yields 12 Muffins
Nutritional Information Per Muffin: 50 calories; 1 gram fat; 9 grams carbohydrates; 1 gram fiber; 2 grams sugar; 2 grams protein

What if you could combine the flavors of pancakes with a fresh baked muffin? I'd say it would be the perfect way to start your morning! Now all of the flavors of a blueberry pancake are packed into a muffin, making it easy to eat on even the busiest of mornings. No fork required!

STRAWBERRY PROTEIN PANCAKE WITH YOGURT FILLING

🕐 Estimated Time: 20 minutes

These pancake roll-ups are a cross between a crepe and a pancake. The best part is that they are packed with protein and healthy whole grains. Although they are sweet enough to be dessert, they are healthy enough to have for breakfast!

Pancakes

1/4 cup plain nonfat Greek yogurt

2 tablespoons vanilla or plain protein powder

1/2 cup old-fashioned oats

1/4 cup chopped strawberries (about 2 large strawberries, rinsed, stems removed, and chopped), plus extra for serving

2 large egg whites

1/8 cup (1 ounce) water

2 to 3 tablespoons sweetener that measures like sugar

1/2 teaspoon baking powder

Yogurt Filling

1/2 cup plain nonfat Greek yogurt

2 tablespoons low-sugar strawberry jam, plus extra for serving

2 to 4 teaspoons sweetener that measures like sugar

Heat a nonstick griddle or large nonstick skillet coated with cooking spray over medium heat. In a blender combine the yogurt, protein powder, oats, strawberries, egg whites, water, sweetener, and baking powder and blend until smooth. Spoon half of the batter onto the preheated griddle. Turn pancake over when tops are covered with bubbles and edges are cooked. Repeat with remaining batter.

In a small bowl stir the yogurt, jam, and sweetener to taste together to make the filling. Divide the filling between the pancakes and roll each pancake up around the filling. Place the roll-ups on a plate seam side down so they stay rolled, or secure with a toothpick. Serve with additional strawberries or low-sugar jam if desired.

Yields 2 Servings
Nutritional Information Per Serving: 187 calories; 2 grams fat; 24 grams carbohydrates; 3 grams fiber; 10 grams sugar; 18 grams protein

GIANT BREAKFAST COOKIE

🕐 Estimated Time: 5 minutes

1/2 cup old-fashioned oats, divided

1 tablespoon protein powder

1 tablespoon low-sugar maple syrup (or agave nectar or honey)

3 tablespoons plain nonfat Greek yogurt

1 to 2 tablespoons sweetener that measures like sugar

1/4 teaspoon baking powder

1/4 teaspoon baking soda

Pinch of salt

1/4 teaspoon ground cinnamon

1 teaspoon mini chocolate chips

Spoon 1/4 cup oats into a blender or food processor and grind into a flour-like consistency. Pour the oat flour into a small bowl and mix together with the remaining 1/4 cup oats, protein powder, syrup, yogurt, sweetener, baking powder, baking soda, salt, and cinnamon. Spray a small microwave-safe plate with cooking spray. Spread the batter onto the plate, forming the batter into a circle with the back of a spoon. Sprinkle chocolate chips on top. Microwave for 1 minute or until cooked. Enjoy immediately or prepare the night before for a quick breakfast.

Yields 1 Serving
Nutritional Information: 197 calories; 3 grams fat; 43 grams carbohydrates; 6 grams fiber; 3 grams sugar; 14 grams protein

No, you're not dreaming. This is actually a giant chocolate chip cookie that is prepared in less than five minutes and can be eaten for breakfast! How is this possible? Well, with the help of our good friend the microwave, this wholesome treat comes together beautifully in one minute! This cookie is awesome for an on-the-go breakfast or as a pre- or post-workout treat. Let's face it, it can be great for any time you're craving a cookie but still want something nutritious. I suggest eating it right off the plate with a spoon!

BANANA BREAD WAFFLES WITH PEANUT BUTTER SYRUP

🕐 Estimated Time: 15 minutes

These banana waffles might be the best breakfast you've ever had! These waffles taste just like a piece of warm, moist banana bread. They have a slight crisp on the outside while being light and fluffy on the inside. Enjoy!

Waffles

1 large banana

1/2 cup low-fat cottage cheese

3 large egg whites

1/4 cup vanilla or plain protein powder

1 cup old-fashioned oats

1/2 teaspoon baking powder

1 to 2 tablespoons sweetener that measures like sugar

Peanut Butter Syrup*

1/4 cup peanut flour

1/4 cup plus 2 tablespoons water

2 teaspoons sweetener that measures like sugar

Pinch of salt

To make the waffles, preheat the waffle maker. In a blender place the banana, cottage cheese, egg whites, protein powder, oats, baking powder, and sweetener and blend until the batter is smooth. Spray the waffle iron with nonstick spray and pour 1/2 cup batter onto the waffle iron when it has reached the appropriate temperature. (The amount of batter used and servings of waffles may vary depending on the size of your waffle maker.) Close the waffle maker and remove the waffle when the "ready" light comes on (or when the waffles are slightly golden brown).

To make the peanut butter syrup, mix together the peanut flour, water, sweetener, and salt until it forms a syrup-like consistency. Add a few more drops of water for a thinner peanut butter syrup, or less water for a thicker peanut butter spread. Pour (or spread) 1 tablespoon of syrup over each waffle. Enjoy warm!

Yields 5 Servings
Nutritional Information Per Serving: 159 calories; 2 grams fat; 22 grams carbohydrates; 4 grams fiber; 6 grams sugar; 15 grams protein

*You could also use 1/4 cup regular peanut butter and melt in the microwave for 30 seconds or until it becomes the liquid consistency of syrup. (Please note that this will change the nutritional information of this recipe.)

STRAWBERRY COFFEE CAKE

🕐 Estimated Time: 35 minutes

3 large egg whites

1/3 cup plain nonfat Greek yogurt

1/2 cup unsweetened almond milk (or low-fat milk)

1 1/2 cups old-fashioned oats

1/2 cup vanilla or plain protein powder

2 teaspoons baking powder

1 teaspoon vanilla extract

1/2 cup sweetener that measures like sugar

1/4 teaspoon salt

1 1/2 cups diced strawberries, divided

Preheat the oven to 350 degrees. Spray a 9 x 9-inch baking dish with cooking spray. In a medium bowl whisk together the egg whites, yogurt, almond milk, oats, protein powder, baking powder, vanilla, sweetener, and salt until everything is well combined. Fold in 1 cup of strawberries. Pour the batter into the prepared baking dish and sprinkle the rest of the strawberries over the top. Bake for 28 to 32 minutes or until a toothpick inserted in the center comes out clean. Cut into 8 portions and serve warm or chilled.

Yields 8 Servings
Nutritional Information Per Serving: 105 calories; 1.5 grams fat; 13 grams carbohydrates; 2 grams fiber; 3 grams sugar; 11 grams protein

I created this recipe specifically with Mother's Day brunch in mind. In my family, we traditionally go to church together and have brunch afterward to celebrate my mom on her special day. This coffee cake turned out moist and flavorful, and it is a delicious way to use up fresh strawberries. It's great for breakfast, brunch, snack, or even dessert.

CINNAMON BUN FOR ONE

⏱ Estimated Time: 5 minutes

One of my husband's favorite breakfast foods is cinnamon buns, but I never like serving him a sugary pastry for the most important meal of the day. So I was on a mission to make a cinnamon bun that was just as healthy as it was delicious. As I thought about how to put together this recipe, I knew it had to have whole grains and protein and be low in sugar. Considering it was for breakfast, it also had to be quick and easy. I'm proud to say this two-minute protein-packed cinnamon bun meets all of these qualifications—and is husband approved!

Cinammon Bun

1/4 cup old-fashioned oats

1 tablespoon vanilla or plain protein powder

2 tablespoons plain nonfat Greek yogurt

1 large egg white

1/2 teaspoon baking powder

2 tablespoons sweetener that measures like sugar

1/4 teaspoon ground cinnamon

Protein-Packed Icing

2 tablespoons plain nonfat Greek yogurt

2 teaspoons sweetener that measures like sugar

Spoon the oats into a blender or food processor and grind into a flour-like consistency. Spray a microwave-safe mug with cooking spray. In a small bowl place the oat flour, protein powder, yogurt, egg white, baking powder, sweetener, and cinnamon and stir until well combined. Pour the batter into the prepared mug and microwave for 1 minute 30 seconds to 2 minutes, or until the cinnamon bun is set.

To make the icing, mix the yogurt with the sweetener in a small bowl. Pour the icing in a zip-top bag and snip the tip of the bottom corner. Swirl the icing onto the cinnamon bun.

Yields 1 Serving
Nutritional Information: 110 calories; 1 gram fat; 12 grams carbohydrates; 1 gram fiber; 1 gram sugar; 13 grams protein

FRENCH TOAST PROTEIN SHAKE

🕐 Estimated Time: 5 minutes

1/2 cup fat-free cottage cheese

1/4 cup vanilla or plain protein powder

1 teaspoon maple extract (or 2 tablespoons low-sugar maple syrup)

1/2 teaspoon ground cinnamon

Dash of ground nutmeg (or pumpkin pie spice)

2 tablespoons sweetener that measures like sugar

1/2 to 1 cup water (alter this according to desired consistency)

5 to 10 ice cubes (use fewer for a thinner consistency)

Place the cottage cheese, protein powder, maple extract, cinnamon, nutmeg, sweetener, water, and ice cubes in a blender and blend until a creamy consistency is reached. Enjoy!

Yields 1 Serving
Nutritional Information: 180 calories; 0 grams fat; 7 grams carbohydrates; 0 grams fiber; 4 grams sugar; 36 grams protein

I have fond childhood memories of the house filling up with the sweet smell of cinnamon while waiting in anticipation for warm French toast that dripped with melted butter and maple syrup. Now you, too, can have all of your favorite flavors whipped up into a thick and creamy protein shake that is so good it could honestly pass as a milkshake. Yes, I did say you could have French toast and a milkshake for breakfast! Now *that* is worth waking up for, if you ask me.

OVERNIGHT FRENCH TOAST BAKE

🕐 Estimated Time: 5 hours or overnight

This French toast is the perfect dish to make when you're planning ahead for breakfast. I make this every year for our Christmas breakfast, and my entire family looks forward to it. It's so easy to make compared to traditional French toast since it is done in one dish. The warm smell of cinnamon and the light crunch of the pecans make this a dish that's sure to please!

2 large eggs

8 large egg whites (or 1 cup liquid egg whites)

1/2 cup low-fat cottage cheese

1/2 cup unsweetened applesauce

1 cup unsweetened almond milk (or low-fat milk)

1 1/2 teaspoons ground cinnamon, divided

1/2 teaspoon salt

1 cup sweetener that measures like sugar

1 teaspoon vanilla extract (or maple extract)

1 cup low-sugar maple syrup (or agave nectar), divided

1 loaf whole grain, high-fiber bread

1/4 cup chopped pecans

Spray a 9 x 13-inch baking dish with cooking spray. In a blender place the eggs, egg whites, cottage cheese, applesauce, almond milk, 1 teaspoon cinnamon, salt, sweetener, vanilla, and 1/2 cup syrup and blend until smooth. Cut the crust off the bread and discard the two end pieces. Cut the bread into small cubes and place in the prepared baking dish. Pour the mixture from the blender over the bread and make sure the egg mixture evenly soaks into all of the bread. Cover the dish with foil and put it in the refrigerator overnight (or for at least 4 hours).

When you're ready to bake your French toast, preheat the oven to 350 degrees. Remove the French toast from the refrigerator and let stand at room temperature for 30 minutes. Just before baking, sprinkle the remaining 1/2 teaspoon cinnamon and pecans over the top of the French toast bake and pour 1/4 cup syrup evenly over the top. Bake uncovered for 50 to 60 minutes or until a knife inserted in the center comes out clean. Pour the remaining 1/4 cup syrup over the French toast bake. Cut into 16 equal pieces and serve warm.

Yields 16 Servings
Nutritional Information Per Serving: 99 calories; 2 grams fat; 14 grams carbohydrates; 2 grams fiber; 2 grams sugar; 8 grams protein

MOCHA JAVA PROTEIN SHAKE

🕐 Estimated Time: 5 minutes

1/2 cup low-fat cottage cheese

1/4 cup vanilla or plain protein powder

1 packet instant coffee (or 1 teaspoon instant coffee powder)

1 tablespoon unsweetened cocoa powder

2 tablespoons half-and-half (or coffee creamer of choice)

2 tablespoons sweetener that measures like sugar, or to taste

1/2 to 1 cup water (alter this according to desired consistency)

5 to 10 ice cubes (use fewer for a thinner consistency)

Add the cottage cheese, protein powder, instant coffee, cocoa powder, half-and-half, sweetener, water, and ice cubes to a blender and blend until a creamy consistency is reached. Enjoy!

Yields 1 Serving
Nutritional Information: 230 calories; 6 grams fat; 9 grams carbohydrates; 2 grams fiber; 3 grams sugar; 41 grams protein

Thick, blended, creamy coffee with a hint of chocolate . . . What is not to love?

COOKIE DOUGH OVERNIGHT OATMEAL

🕐 Estimated Time: 5 minutes

This is one of the easiest, yummiest, and well-balanced breakfasts that can be thrown together the night before and cooked quickly in the morning. There is no longer any excuse for not eating a delicious and satisfying breakfast, no matter how busy your mornings are. This Cookie Dough Overnight Oatmeal is guaranteed to be one of the best meals of your day!

1/2 cup plain nonfat Greek yogurt

3/4 cup unsweetened almond milk (or low-fat milk)

1 cup old-fashioned oats

1/4 cup protein powder (or additional oats)

1/4 cup sweetener that measures like sugar

1 teaspoon chocolate chips

1/2 teaspoon butter extract (or vanilla extract)

1/2 teaspoon ground cinnamon

1/4 teaspoon ground nutmeg

1/8 teaspoon salt

In a medium bowl mix together the yogurt and almond milk. Add the oats, protein powder, sweetener, chocolate chips, butter extract, cinnamon, nutmeg, and salt, and stir to combine. Divide between 2 small bowls, mugs, or mason jars. Cover and refrigerate overnight (or for at least an hour so the oats soften and absorb the liquid). It can be served cold, or microwave for 30 to 60 seconds to enjoy warm.

Yields 2 Servings
Nutritional Information Per Serving: 251 calories; 6 grams fat; 34 grams carbohydrates; 6 grams fiber; 6 grams sugar; 20 grams protein

BAKED CINNAMON DONUTS

🕐 Estimated Time: 15 minutes

....

Donuts

1 cup old-fashioned oats

3/4 cup sweetener that measures like sugar, divided

1/4 teaspoon baking powder

1/8 teaspoon baking soda

1/4 teaspoon salt

1/2 teaspoon ground cinnamon

1/4 cup unsweetened applesauce

1/2 teaspoon maple extract

1/8 cup (1 ounce) unsweetened almond milk (or low-fat milk)

2 large egg whites

Optional Glaze

1/2 cup low-sugar maple syrup

2 tablespoons vanilla or plain protein powder

If you have ever been to a cider mill you probably have fond memories of a warm cinnamon and sugar donut. This version is just as mouthwatering. And they are actually healthy enough to eat for breakfast.

To make the donuts, preheat the oven to 350 degrees. Spray a donut pan with cooking spray. In a blender place the oats, 1/2 cup sweetener, baking powder, baking soda, salt, and cinnamon and blend until the oats are ground into a flour-like consistency. Pour the oat flour mixture into a medium bowl and stir in the applesauce, maple extract, almond milk, and egg whites. Stir to combine. Divide the mixture among 6 donut molds. Bake for 10 to 12 minutes, or until a toothpick inserted in the center of a donut comes out clean.

To make the optional glaze, mix the syrup and protein powder together in a small bowl until the powder is completely dissolved in the syrup. Drizzle over donuts if desired.

Yields 6 Donuts
Nutritional Information Per Donut: 65 calories; 1 gram fat; 11 grams carbohydrates; 2 grams fiber; 1 gram sugar; 3 grams protein

HAM AND EGG MUFFINS

🕐 Estimated Time: 30 minutes

These egg muffins are a delicious way to get your protein and veggies for breakfast. I like to prepare these muffins on a weeknight and have them as breakfast during a busy week. They can be reheated by microwaving a few of them for 30 to 60 seconds.

12 slices thinly sliced ham (or turkey)

2 large eggs

6 large egg whites

1/2 cup finely chopped onion

1/2 cup finely chopped red bell pepper

1/2 cup shredded mozzarella cheese

1 teaspoon salt, or to taste

1/4 teaspoon black pepper, or to taste

Preheat the oven to 350 degrees. Line a 12-cup muffin tin with foil or silicone liners and spray with cooking spray. Place one slice of ham in each muffin cup. (This will form a well for the egg to bake in.) In a medium bowl combine the eggs, egg whites, onions, bell peppers, mozzarella, salt, and pepper. Whisk together until everything is well combined. Fill each muffin cup 3/4 of the way full with the egg mixture. Bake for 25 to 30 minutes or until the eggs are set and cooked through (no longer runny in the center).

Yields 12 Muffins
Nutritional Information Per Muffin: 45 calories; 2 grams fat; 1 gram carbohydrates; 0 grams fiber; 1 gram sugar; 5.5 grams protein

BREAKFAST COOKIES

🕐 Estimated Time: 15 minutes

....

1 3/4 cups old-fashioned oats, divided

1/2 cup protein powder

1/2 cup sweetener that measures like sugar

1/2 teaspoon baking powder

1/2 teaspoon baking soda

1/4 teaspoon ground cinnamon

1/4 teaspoon salt

1/2 ripe banana, mashed

1 large egg

2 tablespoons honey

2 tablespoons plain nonfat Greek yogurt

2 tablespoons chocolate chips

A cookie that is healthy enough to eat for breakfast? Your dreams have finally come true with this breakfast cookie recipe. These cookies are so easy to make and are great for an on-the-go breakfast that will keep you fueled all morning.

Preheat the oven to 350 degrees. Line a baking sheet with foil and spray with cooking spray. Place 3/4 cup oats in a blender or food processor and grind into a flour-like consistency. Pour the oat flour into a medium bowl and mix together with the remaining 1 cup oats, protein powder, sweetener, baking powder, baking soda, cinnamon, and salt.

In a small bowl combine the banana, egg, honey, and yogurt. Spoon the banana mixture into the oat mixture and stir to combine. Add the chocolate chips and stir. Scoop 2 tablespoons of dough and roll into a ball. Press the dough into a round disk on the prepared baking sheet. Repeat until all dough is gone. Bake cookies for 8 to 10 minutes or until cookies are set.

Yields 10 Cookies
Nutritional Information Per Cookie: 114 calories; 2 grams fat; 16 grams carbohydrates; 2 grams fiber; 6 grams sugar; 8 grams protein

SANTA FE STUFFED PEPPER CUPS

🕐 Estimated Time: 40 minutes

These Santa Fe-style stuffed pepper cups are unique in the fact that the bell peppers act as an edible serving dish for the Santa Fe-style eggs. When baked, the peppers become softer (but still slightly crisp) and taste amazing with the Mexican flavors baked inside. Topped with cheese, these Santa Fe Stuffed Pepper Cups are perfect for breakfast, as a snack, or even for dinner!

3 large bell peppers (color of your choice)

1 1/2 cups liquid egg whites (or egg substitute or 8 egg whites)

1/4 cup salsa

1/4 cup black beans

1/4 cup corn

1 cup fresh baby spinach (or 1/2 cup chopped frozen spinach, thawed and squeezed dry)

Pinch of salt

Pinch of black pepper

1/2 cup shredded mozzarella cheese (or low-fat cheese of choice)

Preheat the oven to 425 degrees. Line a baking sheet with foil or parchment paper and spray with cooking spray. Wash the bell peppers and cut around the stem to remove stems. Cut the peppers in half lengthwise and remove the seeds. In a medium bowl mix together the eggs, salsa, beans, corn, spinach, salt, and pepper until well combined. Place the peppers on the prepared baking sheet and pour the egg mixture into the pepper cups, dividing the mixture evenly between the peppers. (If the peppers are leaning, use foil to form a ball and place it under the pepper to help it sit evenly on the pan.) Sprinkle the mozzarella on top of the peppers, dividing it evenly. Bake for 30 to 35 minutes or until the cheese is golden brown.

Yields 6 Servings
Nutritional Information Per Serving: 101 calories; 2 grams fat; 10 grams carbohydrates; 3 grams fiber; 0 grams sugar; 11 grams protein

LUNCH

MINI MEXICAN PIZZAS

🕐 Estimated Time: 20 minutes

Pizzas

4 large whole wheat tortillas, or enough to cut out 12 small circles*

1 1/2 cups extra-lean ground turkey (or lean ground beef), cooked

1/2 cup salsa of choice

2 teaspoons taco seasoning

1/2 cup low-fat refried beans

1/2 cup low-fat shredded Mexican blend (or reduced-fat shredded Cheddar cheese)

Optional Toppings

Salsa

Sliced black olives

Shredded lettuce

Low-fat sour cream

Chopped tomatoes

Preheat the oven to 425 degrees. Spray a 12-cup muffin tin with cooking spray. Start by laying each tortilla on a flat surface. Using an empty can, glass cup, or cookie cutter, cut 3 to 4 medium circles out of each tortilla. Press each circle into a muffin cup using your fingers. (It doesn't have to cover the entire side of the cup; it should just fit snug.)

In a small bowl mix together the ground meat, salsa, taco seasoning, and refried beans. Stir until well combined. Scoop 2 tablespoons of the meat mixture into each tortilla. Top with shredded cheese, dividing evenly between each pizza. Bake for 12 to 15 minutes or until the cheese is melted. Wait for pizzas to cool before removing from the muffin tin using a fork or knife. Pizzas should pop out with ease! Serve with a side of salsa, black olives, lettuce, sour cream, and tomatoes.

Yields 12 Mini Pizzas
Nutritional Information Per Mini Pizza: 80 calories; 3 grams fat; 8 grams carbohydrates; 0 grams sugar; 4 grams fiber; 8 grams protein

* I use La Tortilla wraps.

These mini pizzas are a yummy, well-balanced snack or meal. The refried beans serve as the sauce for these pizzas, which means they are high in fiber. They're also packed with protein, thanks to the ground turkey and cheese. They're so tasty that you'll never believe they're actually good for you.

JALAPEÑO POPPER CHICKEN CHILI

🕐 Estimated Time: 4 or 8 hours

If you enjoy jalapeño chicken poppers as an appetizer or snack, you will love this rich, creamy chili that is popping with all of your favorite flavors. If you prefer a milder version, you can simply swap the jalapeños with diced green chilies. I made this chili for a group of my friends, and it was a crowd pleaser, to say the least. It is simple, delicious, and incredibly satisfying on a chilly day.

1 pound boneless, skinless chicken breasts

1 small onion, diced

1 (4-ounce) can diced jalapeño peppers (or diced green chilies for a milder version)

1 (28-ounce) can diced or chopped tomatoes in juice

2 (15-ounce) cans cannellini beans (or white bean of choice)

1 (15-ounce) can corn, drained

1 (15-ounce) can creamed corn

1/2 teaspoon chili powder, or to taste

1 1/2 teaspoons paprika

1 teaspoon garlic powder

1 teaspoon salt

1/2 teaspoon black pepper

1 cup plain nonfat Greek yogurt (or low-fat cream cheese)

Optional Toppings

Bacon, cooked and crumbled

Green onions, chopped

Spray a 6-quart slow cooker with cooking spray. Place the chicken breasts on the bottom of the slow cooker. In a large bowl stir together onions, jalapeños, tomatoes, beans, corn, creamed corn, chili powder, paprika, garlic powder, salt, and pepper. Spoon the mixture into the slow cooker. Cover and cook on high heat for 4 hours or on low heat for 8 hours. Remove the chicken breasts just before serving and shred with two forks. Return the chicken back to the chili and add the yogurt. Stir to combine. Enjoy with toppings if desired.

Yields 8 Servings (1 1/2 cups per serving)
Nutritional Information Per Serving: 196 calories; 2 grams fat; 23 grams carbohydrates; 6 grams fiber; 4 grams sugar; 21 grams protein

CHICKEN PARMESAN WRAP

🕐 Estimated Time: 5 minutes

1 (4-ounce) cooked chicken breast, cut into strips

1/4 cup spaghetti sauce (or marinara or pizza sauce)*

2 tablespoons grated Parmesan cheese

2 tablespoons shredded mozzarella cheese

1/8 teaspoon Italian seasoning

1/2 cup fresh baby spinach leaves, optional

1 large whole grain or low-carb wrap**

Place the chicken, spaghetti sauce, Parmesan, mozzarella, Italian seasoning, and optional spinach leaves on the wrap. Wrap the bread around the filling and microwave seam side down for 30 to 60 seconds, or until warmed through and the cheese is melted. Enjoy warm!

Yields 1 Serving
Nutritional Information: 262 calories; 9 grams fat; 25 grams carbohydrates; 10 grams fiber; 1 gram sugar; 29 grams protein

* I recommend Classico Tomato & Basil spaghetti sauce with 50 calories per 1/2 cup.

** I use La Tortilla wraps.

If you are looking for a quick and easy lunch, look no further! This chicken Parmesan wrap is so simple to make that it may become one of your favorite ways to eat a sandwich. Everything you love about chicken Parmesan is now wrapped up into a portable and balanced meal that is perfectly portioned for one.

SOUTHWEST QUINOA CHICKEN SALAD

🕐 Estimated Time: 25 minutes

If you have never tried quinoa before, this is the ideal recipe to start with. Quinoa is a seed that looks a lot like couscous and tastes similar to rice, but has a higher level of protein, fiber, and nutrients. It is a great alternative to pasta in almost any recipe. If quinoa seems a bit out of your comfort zone, there is an option to make this salad with whole grain rice, or you can make it grain-free by leaving out the quinoa or rice altogether. This Southwest chicken salad is one of my favorite lunch recipes. It's easy, nutritious, and exploding with traditional Southwest flavors. Not to mention it is loaded with fresh summer vegetables that add flavor and nutrients. You can eat it as is, serve it over greens, stuff it in a pita, or roll it up in a high-fiber tortilla.

1 1/2 cups water

1/2 cup dry quinoa (or whole grain rice)

1 cup diced cooked chicken breast

1 (15-ounce) can black beans, drained and rinsed

1 (15-ounce) can corn, drained

2 plum tomatoes, diced (or 1 cup grape tomatoes, cut in half)

1 small red onion, diced (about 1/2 cup chopped)

1 medium zucchini, diced

1 medium yellow summer squash, diced

1 medium avocado, diced

1/4 teaspoon salt

Pinch of black pepper

2 teaspoons sweetener that measures like sugar

1 tablespoon minced garlic (or 1/2 teaspoon garlic powder)

Juice of 1 lime (or 1 to 2 tablespoons lime juice)

1 bunch cilantro, chopped

Place the water and quinoa in a small saucepan and bring to a boil over high heat. Once it begins to boil, reduce to medium-low and simmer. Cover the saucepan and cook until all the water is absorbed, about 10 minutes. (You will know the quinoa is done when the grain appears soft and translucent.) Remove the pan from the heat and set aside to cool. (If using whole grain rice, cook rice according to the package directions, or skip this step if you are making a grain-free version.)

Once cooled, add the cooked quinoa to a large bowl, add the chicken, beans, corn, tomatoes, onion, zucchini, squash, avocado, salt, pepper, sweetener, garlic, lime juice, and cilantro, and gently toss. Serve immediately, or chill in the refrigerator for 1 hour or overnight to let the flavors fuse together.

Yields 10 Servings with Quinoa (1 cup per serving)
Yields 8 Servings without Quinoa (1 cup per serving)
Nutritional Information Per Serving (with Quinoa): 135 calories; 4 grams fat; 18 grams carbohydrates; 4 grams fiber; 1 gram sugar; 9.5 grams protein
(without Quinoa): 103 calories; 3 grams fat; 12 grams carbohydrates; 3 grams fiber; 1 gram sugar; 8 grams protein

CHICKEN POT PIE MUFFINS

🕐 Estimated Time: 45 minutes

1/2 cup corn

1/2 cup peas (fresh or frozen) (if using frozen, thaw and pat dry)

1/2 cup diced carrots (fresh or frozen) (if using frozen, thaw and pat dry)

1/2 cup old-fashioned oats

1/2 cup grated Parmesan cheese

3 large egg whites

1 1/2 teaspoons poultry seasoning

1/2 teaspoon black pepper

1/2 teaspoon salt

1/2 teaspoon garlic powder

1 pound lean ground chicken (or extra-lean ground turkey)

Preheat the oven to 375 degrees. Spray a 12-cup muffin tin with cooking spray. In a large bowl mix together the corn, peas, carrots, oats, Parmesan, egg whites, poultry seasoning, pepper, salt, and garlic powder. Add the ground chicken and mix with a spoon or your hands until everything is well combined. Scoop 1/3 cup of the mixture into 11 muffin cups. Bake for 35 to 40 minutes or until the ground chicken reaches an internal temperature of at least 165 degrees and is no longer pink in the middle.

Yields 11 Muffins
Nutritional Information Per Muffin: 99 calories; 2 grams fat; 6 grams carbohydrates; 1 gram fiber; 1 gram sugar; 14 grams protein

These Chicken Pot Pie Muffins are a fun spin on a traditional comfort food. Take all of the amazing flavors of chicken pot pie and put them into a perfectly portioned muffin that explodes with flavor and you have a winner! The great thing is, they take very little prep time and freeze well, making this a great recipe for even the busiest person.

SPICY BLACK BEAN BURGERS

🕐 Estimated Time: 35 minutes

These burgers are packed full of flavor and can be enjoyed in many different ways. I enjoy this burger plain, loaded with toppings, or on a lettuce wrap.

2 (15-ounce) cans black beans, drained and rinsed, divided

1/2 cup old-fashioned oats

1/4 cup chopped red onion

2 tablespoons diced jalapeños

1 large egg white

1/2 cup corn (canned or fresh)

1/4 cup shredded mozzarella cheese

1 teaspoon chopped garlic

2 teaspoons sweetener that measures like sugar

1/4 teaspoon salt

Optional Toppings

Thin-sliced Swiss or reduced-fat Cheddar cheese

Low-sugar ketchup

Mustard

Shredded lettuce

Salsa

Preheat the oven to 375 degrees. Line a rimmed baking sheet with foil and spray with cooking spray. In a blender or a food processor combine 1 can of beans, oats, onions, jalapeños, egg white, corn, mozzarella, garlic, sweetener, and salt. Puree until the mixture is smooth (don't overmix). Scoop the mixture into a medium bowl and stir in the remaining can of beans until well combined. Wet your hands, form the mixture into 6 patties, and place on the baking sheet. (The mixture will seem a bit wet, but wet hands should keep it from sticking to you while you shape the patties.) Bake the burgers for 20 to 25 minutes or until firm to the touch. Add a slice of cheese on top of each burger in the last few minutes of cooking if desired. Serve with ketchup, mustard, lettuce, and salsa.

Yields 6 Servings
Nutritional Information Per Serving: 171 calories; 2 grams fat; 34 grams carbohydrates; 9 grams fiber; 2 grams sugar; 11 grams protein

SKINNY SLOPPY JOES

🕐 Estimated Time: 30 minutes or 4 to 8 hours

1 pound extra-lean ground turkey breast

1 small green bell pepper (or 3/4 cup carrots), finely chopped

1 small yellow onion, finely chopped

1/2 teaspoon garlic powder

1 (15-ounce) can pinto beans, drained and rinsed

1 (15-ounce) can tomato sauce

2 teaspoons prepared mustard

1 tablespoon honey

1/4 cup low-sugar ketchup

1 tablespoon sweetener that measures like sugar, optional

8 sandwich thins (or high-fiber buns or wraps)

Cook the ground turkey, bell peppers (or carrots), onions, and garlic powder in a large nonstick skillet over medium-high heat until the meat is browned, breaking up the meat as it cooks, about 4 to 6 minutes. Add the turkey mixture to a 6-quart slow cooker, along with the pinto beans, tomato sauce, mustard, honey, ketchup, and optional sweetener. Cook on high heat for 4 hours or on low heat for 8 hours. Spoon the warm meat on a sandwich thin if desired and enjoy!

Yields 8 Servings
Nutritional Information Per Serving: 130 calories; 2.5 grams fat; 12 grams carbohydrates; 2.5 grams fiber; 5 grams sugar; 15 grams protein

NOTE: This recipe can also be made on the stovetop. Heat a large nonstick skillet over medium-high heat. Spray with cooking spray. Add the onion and peppers (or carrots) and 1/3 cup water. Cook for 4 to 5 minutes, stirring frequently. Stir in the ketchup and cook 2 minutes longer or until the peppers (or carrots) are tender or until the water has evaporated. Add the turkey and cook until it is browned, breaking up the meat as it cooks. Once the meat is browned, stir in the tomato sauce, honey, mustard, garlic powder, beans, and optional sweetener. Reduce heat to low and cook an additional 2 to 5 minutes to blend the flavors. Spoon the warm meat on a sandwich thin and enjoy!

Did you know that the average sloppy joe recipe has up to 17 grams of fat, over 400 calories, and an average of 10 grams of sugar? That may come as a shock, but not to worry! This *Dashing Dish* version has less than 3 grams of fat, only 130 calories, and no added sugar. This recipe has a secret power ingredient packed with fiber, protein, and flavor . . . pinto beans.

CREAMY CHICKEN ENCHILADA SOUP

🕐 Estimated Time: 60 minutes or 4 to 8 hours

Chicken enchiladas are sure to please just about everyone. Put all of these amazing flavors into a creamy soup, and you have a quick and easy meal for a chilly yet busy day! When I served this to my family, they exclaimed that it was by far one of their favorite soup recipes. I hope you and your family enjoy it as much as mine did.

1 pound boneless, skinless chicken breasts

2 (15-ounce) cans diced tomatoes

1 (4-ounce) can chopped green chilies

1 (10-ounce) can enchilada sauce

1 (15-ounce) can corn, drained

1 (15-ounce) can black beans, rinsed and drained

1 cup chicken broth (or 1 chicken bouillon cube plus 1 cup water)

1 medium onion, diced

1 teaspoon chopped garlic (or 1/2 teaspoon garlic powder)

1 tablespoon taco seasoning

1 cup plain nonfat Greek yogurt

Low-fat cheese for topping, optional

Baked chips for serving, optional

Put the chicken, tomatoes, green chilies, enchilada sauce, corn, black beans, broth, onions, garlic, and taco seasoning in a 6-quart slow cooker. Cover and cook on high for 4 hours or low for 8 hours. Take the chicken out of the slow cooker just before serving and shred. Add the chicken back to the soup and stir in the Greek yogurt. Serve warm with cheese and chips if desired.

Yields 12 Servings (1 cup per serving)
Nutritional Information Per Serving: 127 calories; 1 gram fat; 16 grams carbohydrates; 4 grams fiber; 1 gram sugar; 14 grams protein

NOTE: If you don't have a slow cooker, you can make this soup on your stovetop. Place all the ingredients, except for Greek yogurt, in a large pot, cover, and simmer over medium-low heat for 45 to 60 minutes, or until the chicken is cooked through. Take the chicken out of the pot just before serving and shred. Add the chicken back to the soup and stir in the Greek yogurt. Serve warm with cheese and chips if desired.

ASIAN CHICKEN EDAMAME SALAD

🕐 Estimated Time: 10 minutes

Dressing

1 teaspoon minced garlic

1/4 cup reduced-sodium soy sauce

2 tablespoons rice vinegar

1 1/2 tablespoons honey (or 1 teaspoon sweetener that measures like sugar)

Pinch of ground ginger

Salad

1 cup chopped or shredded cooked chicken breast

1 cup shelled edamame beans (cooked according to package directions and cooled)

2 medium bell peppers (red, yellow, or orange), diced

1 cup shredded carrots

4 cups tricolored coleslaw mix

1/2 cup chopped cilantro

3 green onions, chopped, optional

1/4 cup toasted almonds, optional

Optional Topping

1 tablespoon sesame seeds for topping

This is the ultimate power lunch recipe! This salad is extremely quick and easy to make, especially if you use a rotisserie chicken from the grocery store.

Mix the garlic, soy sauce, rice vinegar, honey, and ginger in a small bowl to make the dressing. Place the chicken, edamame, bell peppers, carrots, and coleslaw mix in a large bowl. Toss to combine. Add the dressing to the salad and combine until the salad is fully coated. Add in the cilantro and mix again. Sprinkle green onions and toasted almonds on top if desired. This salad tastes the best when it has chilled for at least 1 hour in the refrigerator or overnight.

Yields 6 Servings (1 cup per serving)
Nutritional Information Per Serving: 120 calories; 2 grams fat; 12 grams carbohydrates; 2 grams fiber; 2 grams sugar; 14 grams protein

CHEESEBURGER LETTUCE WRAPS

⏱ Estimated Time: 25 minutes

These Cheeseburger Lettuce Wraps scream comfort food without the grease that comes along with the typical cheeseburger. The cheeseburger meat filling has the delicious combination of flavors from the sweet ketchup, salty mustard, and Cheddar cheese. This is a melt-in-your-mouth juicy burger that will make it hard to believe how light and fresh these lettuce wraps actually are. The best part about this recipe is that it is very kid friendly while being extremely healthy. This recipe is proof that healthy eating can be fun and delicious!

1 1/4 pounds extra-extra-lean ground turkey (or extra-lean ground beef)

1 medium white onion, diced

3 tablespoons low-sugar ketchup, plus more for wrap

2 tablespoons prepared mustard, plus more for wrap

1/2 teaspoon salt

1/4 teaspoon black pepper

1/2 teaspoon garlic powder

3 tablespoons light mayonnaise (or plain nonfat Greek yogurt), optional

1 teaspoon sweetener that measures like sugar, optional

1/2 cup shredded reduced-fat Cheddar cheese, optional

1 head of lettuce

1 medium tomato, diced, optional

2 dill pickles, diced, optional

Cook ground turkey and diced onions in a large nonstick pan over medium-high heat. Stir and break up the turkey while it is cooking. When the turkey is almost cooked through, add the ketchup, mustard, seasoned salt, pepper, and garlic powder to the pan. Add the mayonnaise and sweetener if desired. (The mayo will add moisture to the meat.) Stir and continue to cook until the ground turkey is completely cooked, about 4 to 6 minutes. Remove the pan from the heat and sprinkle grated Cheddar cheese evenly over the meat while it is still warm if desired.

Cut off the stem (or base) of the lettuce head and cut in half lengthwise. Peel off individual leaves and wash and pat dry. Scoop 1/2 cup meat into each lettuce wrap and serve with tomatoes, pickles, ketchup, and mustard if desired.

Yields 6 Servings (1/2 cup filling for each lettuce wrap)
Nutritional Information Per Serving: 60 calories; 2 grams fat; 1.5 grams carbohydrates; 0.5 grams fiber; 0.5 grams sugar; 8 grams protein

MONTE CRISTO WRAP SANDWICHES

🕐 Estimated Time: 10 minutes

2 high-fiber wraps*

1 teaspoon prepared mustard

2 ounces (about 4 slices) deli ham, thinly sliced

2 ounces (about 4 slices) deli turkey, thinly sliced

2 ultra-thin slices Swiss cheese, cut in half

2 large egg whites

1 ounce unsweetened almond milk (or low-fat milk)

$1/4$ teaspoon salt

1 tablespoon sweetener that measures like sugar

$1/2$ teaspoon ground cinnamon

Dash of powdered sugar for topping, optional

Low-sugar raspberry jam, optional

Lay the wraps out on a flat surface. Spread $1/2$ teaspoon mustard on each wrap. Top each wrap with 2 slices of ham, 2 slices of turkey, and 1 slice of Swiss cheese. Fold each wrap in half. In a small bowl mix the egg whites and almond milk together until well combined and then add the salt, sweetener, and cinnamon. Mix well. Dip both sides of the wrap in the egg mixture just before placing in the pan, making sure both sides of the wrap are coated with the egg mixture (as you would if you were making French toast). This requires both hands to hold the tortilla and all the ingredients inside in place while coating both sides.

Heat a large sauté pan or a large nonstick skillet over medium-low heat. Coat the sauté pan with cooking spray and cook each side of the sandwich until the wrap becomes golden brown on the outside. Remove the wraps from the pan and cut each wrap into 3 triangles. Sprinkle with powdered sugar and serve with raspberry jam for dipping if desired.

Yields 2 Servings
Nutritional Information Per Serving: 297 calories; 7 grams fat; 19.5 grams carbohydrates; 12 grams fiber; 2 grams sugar; 25 grams protein

* I use La Tortilla wraps.

I will never forget the first time I had a Monte Cristo sandwich at a restaurant. I thought to myself, *This must be the most amazing sandwich that ever existed!* It was the perfect combination of sweet and salty, and was almost as good as a dessert. When I started to cook healthy, I decided that this was one meal that I had to re-create at home. I have been making a version of this wrap sandwich for years now, and I think it may be one of my favorite lunches ever. I hope you and your family enjoy it as much as I do.

CHICKEN PARMESAN MUFFINS

🕐 Estimated Time: 50 minutes

Combine the flavors of warm, bubbling cheese, sweet tomato sauce, and salty Parmesan and you are pretty much guaranteed to have a delicious meal. These Chicken Parmesan Muffins are prepared in a muffin tin, which takes all of the guesswork out of the portion size, and makes them kid friendly as well.

5 ounces fresh spinach (or 1 cup frozen spinach, thawed and squeezed dry)

1 small onion, finely chopped

1 teaspoon minced garlic (or $1/2$ teaspoon garlic powder)

1 pound lean ground chicken (or extra-lean ground turkey or ground beef)

$1/2$ cup liquid egg whites (or 2 large eggs)

1 cup canned diced tomatoes, drained (I used one with basil, garlic, and oregano)

$1/4$ cup old-fashioned oats

$3/4$ cup grated Parmesan cheese, divided

$1/2$ teaspoon dried basil

$1/2$ teaspoon dried oregano

$1/8$ teaspoon salt

Pinch of black pepper

1 cup marinara or spaghetti sauce*

Fresh or dried parsley for garnish, optional

Preheat the oven to 350 degrees. Line a 12-cup muffin tin with foil or silicone liners and spray with cooking spray. (You could also use a loaf pan if you prefer to make this recipe into a meatloaf.) In a small sauté pan cook the spinach, onions, and garlic over medium heat until the onions are translucent. Let cool to room temperature.

In a large bowl combine the ground chicken, spinach mixture, egg whites, diced tomatoes, oats, $1/2$ cup Parmesan, basil, oregano, salt, and pepper. Don't overmix or the meat will get tough. Divide the mixture among the muffin cups (about $1/4$ cup per muffin cup) or put the mixture in a loaf pan. Top each muffin with 2 tablespoons of the marinara sauce. Divide the remaining $1/4$ cup Parmesan among the 12 muffins.

Bake for 35 to 40 minutes (or 45 to 55 minutes for a loaf pan), or until each meatloaf reaches an internal temperature of 165 degrees and is no longer pink in the middle. Remove from the oven and allow the meat to rest for 5 minutes before slicing or serving. Garnish with parsley if desired.

Yields 12 Muffins
Nutritional Information Per Muffin: 107 calories; 3.5 grams fat; 5 grams carbohydrates; 1 gram fiber; 2 grams sugar; 14 grams protein

* I recommend Classico Tomato & Basil spaghetti sauce with 50 calories per $1/2$ cup.

GREEK CHICKEN LETTUCE WRAPS

🕐 Estimated Time: 25 minutes

2 tablespoons lemon juice

1/4 cup balsamic vinegar

2 tablespoons red wine vinegar

1 tablespoon honey

2 tablespoons water (or olive oil)

1 teaspoon dried oregano

1/2 teaspoon onion powder

1/2 teaspoon garlic powder

1 pound boneless, skinless chicken breasts

1 medium zucchini, finely diced

1 medium red bell pepper, finely diced

1/2 cup diced red onion

8 grape (or cherry) tomatoes, halved

1/2 cup chickpeas (or garbanzo beans)

1/4 cup crumbled feta cheese

1 large head iceberg lettuce

1/3 cup plain nonfat Greek yogurt, optional

Fresh parsley, optional

These Greek Chicken Lettuce Wraps are exploding with fresh flavors. They are quick to make and the filling is extremely versatile. You can prepare this recipe in various ways by swapping the lettuce wraps with a low-carb wrap, sprinkle the filling over a bed of lettuce, or eat the filling as is!

In a small bowl mix the lemon juice, balsamic vinegar, red wine vinegar, honey, water, oregano, onion powder, and garlic powder. In a large sauté pan coated with cooking spray cook the chicken over medium-high heat until it begins to turn white on the outside (about 2 minutes) and add 1/2 of the vinaigrette to the pan. Continue to cook until the chicken is cooked through (about 5 additional minutes) and the vinaigrette has evaporated. Remove the pan from the heat and pour the chicken into a large bowl. If you prefer the zucchini, bell peppers, and red onions to be cooked, add them to the sauté pan and cook for 2 to 4 minutes, or until the zucchini becomes soft and the onions become translucent.

In a medium bowl combine the zucchini, bell peppers, onions, tomatoes, chickpeas, and feta with the remaining vinaigrette and stir to combine. Add the toppings to the cooked chicken and stir to combine. Toss salad with yogurt and parsley just before serving if desired.

To make the lettuce wraps, cut off the stem (or base) of the lettuce head and cut in half lengthwise. Peel off individual leaves and wash and pat dry. Scoop $^1/_2$ cup of the mixture in each lettuce wrap and top with a dollop of yogurt and fresh parsley if desired.

Yields 12 Servings ($^1/_2$ cup filling for each lettuce wrap)
Nutritional Information Per Serving: 83 calories; 2 grams fat; 5 grams carbohydrates; 1 gram fiber; 1 gram sugar; 11 grams protein

LIGHTENED UP SALMON CAKES

🕐 Estimated Time: 20 minutes

Although I have always enjoyed salmon cakes, I steered away from making them at home because they seemed intimidating. As I always try to do with my recipes, I have simplified this recipe so that it is quick and easy to make. These salmon cakes are so moist and flavorful that you may have a hard time believing they are actually healthy! This recipe is restaurant-quality without all of the fuss.

2 (5-ounce) cans pink salmon, drained and squeezed dry (or 10 ounces baked salmon, flaked)

1/2 cup old-fashioned oats (or panko bread crumbs)

1/2 cup grated Parmesan cheese (or additional oats or bread crumbs)

1/2 cup corn

1/4 cup finely chopped red onion

1/4 cup finely chopped red bell pepper

1/2 teaspoon garlic powder (or 1 teaspoon minced garlic)

2 large eggs

Pinch of salt

Pinch of black pepper

Preheat the oven to 400 degrees. Line a rimmed baking sheet with foil or parchment paper and spray with cooking spray. (To get the salmon cakes extra crispy on both sides, you can place a wire cooling rack in the baking sheet and spray with cooking spray.) In a small bowl combine salmon, oats, Parmesan, corn, onions, bell peppers, garlic powder, eggs, salt, and black pepper and mix well. Shape the salmon mixture into 6 cakes, each about 3/4 inch thick, and place on the prepared baking sheet. Bake for 10 to 15 minutes until the tops are lightly golden brown or until the salmon cakes are slightly firm to the touch.

Yields 6 Servings
Nutritional Information Per Serving: 128 calories; 4 grams fat; 8 grams carbohydrates; 1 gram fiber; 0.5 grams sugar; 14 grams protein

INSIDE-OUT PHILLY CHEESESTEAK PEPPERS

🕐 Estimated Time: 30 minutes

4 large green bell peppers

1 medium white onion, diced or cut into strips

1 (8-ounce) package mushrooms, sliced (or veggie of choice)

1 cup beef broth (or chicken broth), divided

1 teaspoon minced garlic (or 1/2 teaspoon garlic powder)

1 pound extra-lean ground turkey (or lean ground beef or lean sirloin steak, cut into thin strips)

1/8 teaspoon salt

Pinch of black pepper

3/4 cup steak sauce, plus extra for serving

12 slices ultra-thin Swiss cheese (or ultra-thin provolone cheese), divided

A traditional Philly cheesesteak sandwich contains chopped steak, melted cheese, green bell peppers, and onions, all packed inside a bun. I have turned this sandwich inside out, replacing the bun with a green bell pepper. The filling is packed with all the big flavors of caramelized onions and sautéed mushrooms. You won't miss a thing with this amazing spin on the traditional Philly sandwich!

Preheat the oven to 425 degrees. Spray a 9 x 13-inch baking pan with cooking spray (or for easy cleanup, line the pan with foil and spray with cooking spray). Slice the bell peppers in half lengthwise. Remove and discard the seeds and place the halves on the baking pan. Place a large sauté pan over medium-high heat and spray with cooking spray. Add onions, mushrooms, 1/2 cup of beef broth, and garlic and cook until the broth has evaporated and the onions are tender. Place the mixture in a large bowl and set aside.

Put the ground meat in the sauté pan and add the remaining 1/2 cup broth, salt, and black pepper to the pan. Cook over medium-high heat, stirring frequently, until the meat is cooked through, 4 to 6 minutes or until the meat is no longer pink. Remove the pan from the heat and spoon the meat into the onion and mushroom mixture. Add the steak sauce and 4 pieces of cheese and stir until the cheese just begins to melt.

Fill each bell pepper with the meat mixture. Top each bell pepper with a slice of cheese. Bake for 15 to 20 minutes until the cheese is golden brown. Enjoy with a side of steak sauce if desired.

Yields 8 Servings
Nutritional Information Per Serving: 180 calories; 5.5 grams fat; 12 grams carbohydrates; 1 gram fiber; 3 grams sugar; 20 grams protein

SLOW COOKER CHICKEN CORN CHOWDER

⏱ Estimated Time: 4 or 8 hours

What could be better than a bowl of warm chicken corn chowder that has the flavors of sweet corn paired with the saltiness of bacon and cheese? Traditional corn chowder is made with potatoes and heavy cream, but with the creaminess of the Greek yogurt and my favorite mock potato ingredient (cauliflower), this recipe is just as rich as the real thing. This chowder is an easy and tasty meal that makes plenty of leftovers for a quick lunch or dinner throughout the week. When served with chicken (either mixed in or as a side), it makes a well-rounded meal on a chilly day.

1/2 pound boneless, skinless chicken breasts

1 small yellow onion, chopped

1/2 cup chopped carrots

3 stalks celery, roughly chopped

1 medium red bell pepper, roughly chopped

1 medium head cauliflower, washed and cut into 1/4-inch pieces

2 cups chicken broth

1 (15-ounce) can corn, drained

Pinch of salt

Pinch of black pepper

1/2 cup shredded reduced-fat Cheddar cheese

1/4 cup grated Parmesan cheese

1 cup low-fat plain Greek yogurt (or fat-free sour cream)

Add the chicken, onions, carrots, celery, bell peppers, cauliflower, chicken broth, corn, salt, and black pepper to a 6-quart slow cooker. Cover and cook on high for 4 hours or on low for 8 hours. After cooking, remove the chicken breasts from the slow cooker and place on a cutting board. Shred the chicken with two forks and set aside. Meanwhile, ladle or pour the rest of the contents from the slow cooker into a blender. Blend until just smooth (or completely smooth if you prefer a smoother consistency). Pour the chowder back into the slow cooker and stir in the shredded chicken, Cheddar, Parmesan, and yogurt until everything is well combined.

Yields 12 Servings (1 cup per serving)
Nutritional Information Per Serving: 89 calories; 2 grams fat; 10 grams carbohydrates; 2 grams fiber; 1 gram sugar; 9 grams protein

SKINNY EGG SALAD

🕐 Estimated Time: 15 minutes

3 large eggs

1 slice center-cut bacon (or turkey bacon) cooked and crumbled

1/2 stalk celery, coarsely chopped

Chives or green onions, chopped fine, optional

Sweet pickles, chopped fine, optional

2 tablespoons plain nonfat Greek yogurt

1 tablespoon light mayonnaise (or additional Greek yogurt)

1/2 teaspoon prepared mustard

Pinch of salt to taste

Pinch of black pepper to taste

Pinch of paprika, optional

I always like to have hardboiled eggs in the fridge for a quick and easy snack or a healthy lunch. This is a skinny version of egg salad that is packed with protein and bursting with flavor.

Place the eggs in a medium saucepan and cover them with cold water. (Be sure the tops of the eggs are covered by at least an inch of water.) Bring the water to a full boil uncovered and then turn the heat down to medium so that the water is simmering, but not boiling. Let the eggs cook over medium heat for 15 minutes, then remove the pan from the heat. Immediately place the pan in the sink and run cold water into the pan, letting the cold water run over the eggs for about 3 minutes. Remove the boiled eggs from the pot and peel.

To make the egg salad, peel the eggs and separate 2 egg whites from the yolks. Use a fork to coarsely chop one whole egg and the two egg whites coarsely in a medium bowl. Add the bacon, celery, and chives or green onions, and sweet pickles if desired. In a small bowl mix together the yogurt, mayonnaise, mustard, salt, and pepper. Gently stir the dressing into the bowl with the eggs. Add paprika if desired. Chill and enjoy.

Yields 2 Servings (1/2 cup per serving)
Nutritional Information Per Serving: 90 calories; 3 grams fat; 1 gram carbohydrates; 0 grams fiber; 1 gram sugar; 9 grams protein

TEN-MINUTE TACO SALAD

🕐 Estimated Time: 10 minutes

This taco salad is one of my favorite go-to meals when I'm short on time but still want to make something packed with flavor that is also very filling. Traditional taco salads are typically served in a taco bowl, which can pack as many as 500 calories and 20 grams of fat just for the bowl! I re-created the taco bowl in a simple way, which only adds 100 calories and makes this taco salad fun to eat. (You could also skip this step and serve this salad in a regular bowl as well.)

1 (15-ounce) can corn, drained

1 low-carb wrap*

1/2 cup extra-lean ground turkey, fully cooked

1/4 cup taco sauce

2 cups shredded lettuce

1/4 cup salsa

1 tablespoon plain nonfat Greek yogurt

1/4 cup reduced-fat shredded cheese, optional

1/4 cup black beans, optional

1/8 cup black olives, optional

Preheat the oven to 450 degrees. Spoon 1/4 cup corn into a small bowl and pour the remaining corn into another container and refrigerate until ready to use in another dish. After removing the corn from the can, remove the paper from the can and place the can on a baking sheet. Drape the wrap over the can and place in the oven for 6 to 8 minutes, or until the tortilla is golden brown and crispy. (You could also use any empty can you have on hand or an oven-safe mug or dish that you can drape the wrap over.)

While the tortilla is baking, mix together the meat and taco sauce in a small bowl and stir until combined. Remove the tortilla from the oven and allow to cool. Carefully take it off the can and flip it over to make your bowl. Add the lettuce, followed by the meat, corn, salsa, and yogurt. If desired, add shredded cheese, black beans, and black olives. Serve immediately.

Yields 1 Serving
Nutritional Information: 300 calories; 8 grams fat; 44 grams carbohydrates; 17 grams fiber; 5 grams sugar; 24 grams protein

* I use La Tortilla wraps.

LOW-CARB PIZZA QUESADILLA

🕐 Estimated Time: 10 minutes

2 tablespoons pizza sauce, plus extra for serving

1 high-fiber, low-carb wrap* or flatbread

1/2 teaspoon Italian or pizza seasoning

4 ounces thinly sliced ham or turkey deli meat

1/4 cup shredded mozzarella cheese (or 1 cheese stick)

1 tablespoon grated Parmesan cheese

3 to 4 turkey pepperonis (microwaved on a paper towel for 30 seconds until crisp), optional

Preheat a Panini grill or a sauté pan over medium-high heat and spray with cooking spray. Spread the pizza sauce on half of the wrap. Sprinkle Italian seasoning over the sauce and add the deli meat to the bread. Sprinkle the mozzarella on top of the meat layer (or pull apart string cheese and lay on the bread), and finish by sprinkling the Parmesan on top. Add the pepperonis if desired.

Fold the bread in half over the meat and cheese. Place the sandwich in the Panini grill or prepared sauté pan and cook until the sandwich is golden brown and toasted on both sides and the cheese is melted. (If using a sauté pan, you will need to flip the sandwich to toast both sides. A Panini grill will take care of both sides at once.) Use a pizza cutter to cut into wedges if desired. Serve warm and with a side of pizza sauce for dipping if desired.

Yields 1 Serving
Nutritional Information: 223 calories; 6 grams fat; 24 grams carbohydrates; 12 grams fiber; 4 grams sugar; 29 grams protein

* I use La Tortilla wraps.

This recipe is so simple yet delicious. I love quesadillas for lunch because they make a quick and balanced lunch that is ready in minutes. This pizza quesadilla tastes like a fresh slice of pizza combined with a warm and cheesy quesadilla.

PERSONAL THAI CHICKEN PIZZA

🕐 Estimated Time: 20 minutes

Have you ever been in the mood for take-out food but you can't decide what to order? Before you answer that question, put down the phone. This personal pan pizza is the best of both worlds . . . pizza and Thai! Even more amazing, this pizza is less than 300 calories and is packed with fiber and protein to keep you satisfied. This spin on pizza may just be your new favorite way to enjoy a quick and healthy meal that is ready before take-out would be at your door.

1 whole grain pita (or low-carb tortilla)*

3 tablespoons peanut flour, or 1 tablespoon peanut butter, microwaved for 20 to 30 seconds or until peanut butter is melted

2 tablespoons water**

1/2 teaspoon rice wine vinegar

1/2 teaspoon reduced-sodium soy sauce

1 teaspoon sweetener that measures like sugar

1/4 cup shredded cooked chicken

1/4 cup mozzarella cheese

1 tablespoon sliced green onions

1/8 cup chopped cilantro, optional

1/8 cup chopped peanuts, optional

Preheat the oven to 450 degrees. Line a rimmed baking sheet with foil and spray with cooking spray. Place the pita on the baking sheet.

To make the peanut sauce, in a small bowl whisk together the peanut flour, water, rice wine vinegar, soy sauce, and sweetener. Spread 3/4 of the peanut sauce mixture on the pita, leaving a 1/2-inch edge. Sprinkle the shredded chicken on top, followed by the mozzarella. Bake for 12 to 15 minutes, or until the cheese is melted. (About halfway through the cooking time, check the pizza and cover the edges of the crust with foil so they don't burn.) Remove the pizza from the oven and top with green onions, cilantro, and chopped peanuts if desired. Drizzle the remaining peanut sauce on top and serve immediately.

Yields 1 Serving
Nutritional Information (with Peanut Flour): 277 calories; 8.5 grams fat; 16 grams carbohydrates; 7 grams fiber; 1 gram sugar; 23 grams protein; **(with Peanut Butter):** 296 calories; 14.5 grams fat; 14 grams carbohydrates; 6 grams fiber; 2.5 grams sugar; 18 grams protein

* I use Joseph's pitas or La Tortilla wraps.

** Omit this ingredient if using peanut butter instead of peanut flour.

DINNER

DEEP-DISH SPAGHETTI PIZZA PIE

🕐 Estimated Time: 1 hour 15 minutes

1 small to medium spaghetti squash (2 cups cooked)

1/4 cup skim milk (or low-fat milk of choice)

2 large egg whites

1/2 cup low-fat cottage cheese

1/2 teaspoon garlic powder

1/2 teaspoon onion powder

1/4 teaspoon salt

1/4 teaspoon black pepper

1/2 teaspoon Italian seasoning (or 1/4 teaspoon each of basil and oregano)

1 teaspoon sweetener that measures like sugar

1 1/4 cups cooked extra-extra-lean ground turkey

1 cup spaghetti sauce*

1/4 cup shredded mozzarella cheese

This dish is a great way to put a delicious spin on a traditional spaghetti dinner. It's simple, delicious, and a yummy combination of pizza and spaghetti. The unique thing about this version is that the dish doesn't use any spaghetti noodles at all. This spaghetti pizza pie uses spaghetti squash, which is much healthier. The crust comes out slightly browned with crispy edges, and the warm sauce and cheese truly top off this amazing dish. It can be prepared the night before and baked the next day for a quick and easy weeknight dinner.

Preheat the oven to 425 degrees. Spray a round cake pan (or 8 x 8-inch pan) with cooking spray. Pierce the spaghetti squash with a knife to release the steam while cooking. Microwave for 5 to 10 minutes or until soft. Cut the spaghetti squash in half and discard the seeds. Remove 2 packed cups of the "spaghetti" noodles from the squash and blot dry with a kitchen towel to remove excess moisture. Place squash noodles in a large bowl.

Add the milk, egg whites, cottage cheese, garlic power, onion powder, salt, pepper, Italian seasoning, and sweetener to the squash and mix until well combined. Microwave the mixture for 1 minute, stir, and microwave for 1 additional minute. Spoon the mixture into the prepared pan and bake for 30 to 35 minutes and remove from oven. Reduce the oven temperature to 375 degrees.

To make the topping, mix the ground turkey with the spaghetti sauce. Spread the spaghetti sauce and meat mixture over squash mixture and sprinkle with the mozzarella. Return to oven and bake until cheese is bubbly, about 25 to 30 minutes.

Yields 8 Servings
Nutritional Information Per Serving: 72 calories; 2 grams fat; 5 grams carbohydrates; 1 gram fiber; 1 gram sugar; 9 grams protein

* I recommend Classico Tomato & Basil spaghetti sauce with 50 calories per 1/2 cup.

CREAMY BUFFALO CHICKEN ENCHILADAS

🕐 Estimated Time: 35 minutes

The filling for these buffalo chicken enchiladas is so creamy that you will never believe it is actually healthy. Whether you make them for a weeknight with the family or for a football game, these buffalo chicken enchiladas will mean one happy crowd!

1 (14-ounce) can mild enchilada sauce

1/2 cup buffalo wing sauce*

1 1/2 cups shredded cooked chicken

1/2 cup nonfat Greek yogurt (or low-fat sour cream)

1/4 teaspoon garlic powder

1 (15-ounce) can great Northern beans, drained, rinsed, and mashed with a fork

10 high-fiber, low-carb tortillas**

3/4 cup shredded mozzarella cheese

1/4 cup chopped green onions

1/4 cup chopped fresh cilantro, optional

1/4 cup crumbled feta cheese (or blue cheese), optional

Preheat the oven to 350 degrees. Spray an 8 x 10-inch baking dish with cooking spray. In a medium bowl mix together the enchilada sauce and buffalo wing sauce. In a large bowl toss together the shredded chicken, yogurt, garlic powder, and beans. Pour in 1/2 cup of the sauce mixture and stir until combined. Fill each tortilla with 1/3 to 1/2 cup of the chicken mixture. Roll the tortilla and place it seam side down in the dish. Once all tortillas are filled, pour the remaining sauce mixture on top of the tortillas. Top the enchiladas with the mozzarella and bake for 20 to 25 minutes uncovered, or until the cheese is melted and the sauce is bubbling. Immediately after taking the enchiladas out of the oven, top with the green onions, cilantro, and feta cheese if desired and serve warm.

Yields 10 Servings
Nutritional Information Per Serving: 188 calories; 6 grams fat; 26 grams carbohydrates; 15 grams fiber; 1 gram sugar; 21 grams protein

* I like Frank's Red Hot Buffalo Wing Sauce.

** I like La Tortilla wraps.

ITALIAN-STYLE STUFFED RED PEPPERS

🕐 Estimated Time: 45 minutes

3 red bell peppers

1 pound extra-lean ground turkey (or lean ground beef)

2 cups spaghetti sauce*

1 teaspoon basil and oregano seasoning (or any blend of Italian herbs)

1 teaspoon garlic powder

1/2 teaspoon salt

1/2 teaspoon black pepper

1 teaspoon sweetener that measures like sugar, optional

1/2 cup frozen chopped spinach (or veggie of choice), thawed and squeezed dry

1/2 cup grated Parmesan cheese, divided**

I love the taste of a rich marinara or spaghetti sauce. The only problem is most foods that use a red sauce are heavy pasta dishes. I decided to change that by using my favorite turkey meat sauce and stuffing it in a red pepper. These stuffed red peppers are quick and simple to make for a weeknight dinner or to pack for lunch the next day.

Preheat the oven to 450 degrees. Line a rimmed baking sheet with foil and spray with cooking spray. Wash the bell peppers and cut around the stem and remove. Cut the bell peppers in half lengthwise and remove the seeds and ribs inside the bell peppers. Set the bell pepper halves on the baking sheet.

Cook the ground turkey in a large nonstick pan over medium-high heat. Stir and break up the turkey while it is cooking, about 4 to 6 minutes. When the turkey is almost completely cooked, add the spaghetti sauce, basil and oregano seasoning, garlic, salt, black pepper, and optional sweetener to the pan. Stir to combine. Add the spinach and 4 tablespoons Parmesan and stir until everything is well combined. Scoop 1/2 cup of the turkey mixture into each bell pepper. Sprinkle 1 tablespoon Parmesan over each bell pepper. Bake for 20 to 30 minutes or until the cheese has melted and is lightly golden brown.

Yields 6 Servings
Nutritional Information Per Serving: 170 calories; 8 grams fat; 10 grams carbohydrates; 3 grams fiber; 2 grams sugar; 19 grams protein

* I recommend Classico Tomato & Basil spaghetti sauce with 50 calories per 1/2 cup.

** You can substitute another low-fat shredded cheese for the Parmesan cheese.

PIZZA STUFFED CHICKEN BREASTS

◷ Estimated Time: 45 minutes

If you love pizza, these Pizza Stuffed Chicken Breasts are going to knock your socks off! I took all the amazing things about pizza and stuffed it into a chicken breast. Now you get all the flavors of a piece of pizza and the extra protein from the chicken, without all of the empty calories!

1 1/4 pounds (about 4 chicken breasts) boneless, skinless chicken breasts

1/2 cup shredded mozzarella cheese

1/2 cup pizza (or pasta) sauce, divided

1/4 teaspoon salt

1/4 teaspoon black pepper

1/2 teaspoon garlic powder

1 teaspoon Italian seasoning

12 turkey pepperonis

Preheat the oven to 375 degrees. Prepare a rimmed baking sheet with foil and spray with cooking spray. Place each chicken breast between plastic wrap or in a large zip-top bag and pound thin using a mallet or rolling pin. Lay the chicken out on the prepared baking sheet. In a small bowl mix together the mozzarella, pizza sauce, salt, pepper, garlic powder, and Italian seasoning. Spread about 1/4 of the mixture evenly over each chicken breast. Roll up each breast and place seam side down on the baking sheet. Pour the remaining pizza sauce over the top of the chicken breasts and place 3 pepperonis on top of each chicken breast. Bake for 30 to 35 minutes or until the chicken is cooked through or a meat thermometer registers a minimum of 165 degrees.

Yields 4 Servings
Nutritional Information Per Serving: 180 calories; 5 grams fat; 5 grams carbohydrates; 1 gram fiber; 3 grams sugar; 30 grams protein

NO NOODLE LASAGNA

🕐 Estimated Time: 1 hour 30 minutes

....

Noodles

6 large zucchini, cut lengthwise into 1/8-inch strips*

Pinch of salt

Pinch of black pepper

Meat Sauce

1 1/4 pounds extra-lean ground turkey

1 large onion, diced

2 cups fresh or frozen chopped broccoli

2 cups fresh or frozen chopped cauliflower

2 cups fresh or frozen chopped spinach (if using frozen, thaw and squeeze dry)

2 tablespoons Italian seasoning

1 tablespoon garlic powder

Pinch of salt

Pinch of black pepper

1 (25-ounce) jar spaghetti sauce**

Cheese Layer

1 (16-ounce) container low-fat cottage cheese or low-fat ricotta cheese

1/2 cup grated Parmesan cheese

Topping

3/4 cup shredded mozzarella cheese

I love the taste of lasagna, but the heavy amount of starchy carbs and greasy cheese often leave me with a sluggish feeling. I created this veggie-filled variation that has all the wonderful textures and flavors of traditional lasagna, without the heavy after-effects.

To make the noodles, preheat the oven to 425 degrees. Spray a rimmed baking sheet with cooking spray and arrange the zucchini slices on the sheet and season with salt and pepper. Bake for 5 minutes on each side. Set the zucchini slices aside and lower the oven temperature to 375 degrees.

To make the meat sauce: In a large nonstick skillet cook the ground turkey over medium-high heat until it is cooked through, breaking up the meat as it cooks, 5 to 7 minutes. Remove the meat from the pan and place in a large bowl. In the skillet place the onions, broccoli, cauliflower, spinach, Italian seasoning, garlic powder, salt, pepper, and spaghetti sauce and simmer for about 10 minutes or until the veggies begin to get tender or are thawed, stirring occasionally. Add the cooked vegetables to the bowl with the ground meat and stir to combine.

To make the cheese layer, mix the cottage cheese

and Parmesan together (this can be done right in the cottage cheese container).

To assemble the dish, spray a 9 x 13-inch baking dish with cooking spray. Begin by spreading $1/2$ of the meat sauce in the bottom of the prepared dish. Place a layer of zucchini slices on top of the meat, followed by a layer of cottage cheese mixture. Repeat this layering process twice, ending with the cottage cheese layer. Sprinkle the mozzarella evenly over the top. Cover with foil and bake for 1 hour. Remove the foil and bake or broil another 5 minutes until the cheese is browned. Remove the pan from the oven and let rest for about 10 minutes before slicing.

Yields 8 Servings
Nutritional Information Per Serving: 300 calories; 13 grams fat; 30 grams carbohydrates; 8 grams fiber; 13 grams sugar; 34 grams protein

* If you don't want to use zucchini for the noodles, you could use a large eggplant cut lengthwise into $1/8$-inch strips, or 1 box no-boil lasagna noodles.

** I recommend Classico Tomato & Basil spaghetti sauce with 50 calories per $1/2$ cup.

APPLE BACON FETA TURKEY SLIDERS

🕐 Estimated Time: 45 minutes

Apple, bacon, and feta cheese were destined to be married together in one recipe. Add the sweetness of maple syrup (or honey or barbecue sauce) and you have a sweet and salty explosion of flavors bursting in your mouth with these moist and flavorful turkey sliders.

1 pound extra-lean ground turkey (or lean ground beef)

2 slices center-cut bacon, cooked and crumbled

1/2 cup finely diced apple

1/4 cup finely diced sweet onion

1/3 cup crumbled feta cheese

4 tablespoons low-sugar maple syrup (or low-sugar barbecue sauce)

1/2 teaspoon salt

1/4 teaspoon black pepper

1/2 teaspoon garlic powder

1/2 teaspoon poultry seasoning, optional

9 whole grain buns, sandwich thins, or lettuce wraps, optional, for serving

Preheat the oven to 425 degrees. Line a rimmed baking sheet with foil and spray with cooking spray. In a large bowl mix the turkey, bacon, apples, onions, feta, syrup (or barbecue sauce), salt, pepper, garlic powder, and optional poultry seasoning together until combined. (I like to use my hands to mix everything well.) Scoop 1/4 cup of the meat mixture and form into 9 mini sliders. Place the sliders on the prepared baking sheet. Bake for 30 to 35 minutes or until the centers of the burgers are no longer pink or a meat thermometer reaches a minimum of 165 degrees. Remove the baking sheet from the oven and let the burgers rest for 5 to 10 minutes. Serve on a whole grain bun, sandwich thin, or lettuce wrap if desired.

Yields 9 Servings
Nutritional Information Per Serving: 100 calories; 5 grams fat; 2 grams carbohydrates; 0.5 grams fiber; 1 gram sugar; 12 grams protein

THREE-CHEESE CHICKEN PASTA BAKE

🕐 Estimated Time: 55 minutes

2 cups dry high-fiber penne pasta or whole wheat penne pasta

1 cup plain nonfat Greek yogurt

1 cup low-fat cottage cheese

1 cup spaghetti sauce*

1 whole large egg plus 1 large egg white, beaten

3/4 cup grated Parmesan cheese, divided

1 cup shredded mozzarella cheese, divided

1 teaspoon garlic powder

1 tablespoon dried parsley

1/2 teaspoon salt

1 1/2 cups chopped or shredded cooked chicken breast

Preheat the oven to 350 degrees. Spray a 9 x 13-inch baking dish with cooking spray. Fill a medium pot with water and bring to a boil over high heat. Salt the water liberally, lower the heat to medium-high, and add the pasta. Cook until tender, 7 to 10 minutes. Drain and set aside.

In a large bowl stir together the yogurt, cottage cheese, spaghetti sauce, egg and egg white, 1/2 cup Parmesan, 1/4 cup mozzarella, garlic powder, parsley, and salt. Add the chicken and pasta to the sauce and toss to combine. Pour the pasta mixture into the baking dish and spread evenly. Top evenly with remaining 1/4 cup Parmesan and 3/4 cup mozzarella. Bake for 35 to 40 minutes or until the cheese is melted.

Yields 12 Servings (1 cup per serving)
Nutritional Information Per Serving: 154 calories; 5 grams fat; 6.5 grams carbohydrates; 2 grams fiber; 2 grams sugar; 22 grams protein

* I recommend Classico Tomato & Basil spaghetti sauce with 50 calories per 1/2 cup.

Not many people associate the terms *pasta bake* or *three cheese* with healthy, but look no further. This dish is all that and more! This pasta bake is easy to prepare and perfect for weeknight family dinners and weekend entertaining. It is a balanced meal that is guaranteed to please even the pickiest of eaters.

SLOW COOKER SWEET AND SOUR CHICKEN

Estimated Time: 3 or 6 hours

Take-out is generally anything but healthy, especially when it comes to fried and battered sweet and sour chicken. This light and healthy sweet and sour chicken has all of the amazing flavors of your favorite sauce, but in a much healthier way. So the next time you are tempted to make that call for take-out, gather your ingredients and make this at-home version that will leave you feeling satisfied.

1 pound boneless, skinless chicken breast (or lean turkey, pork, or beef)

2 tablespoons cider vinegar

1 tablespoon reduced-sodium soy sauce

1/4 cup low-sugar ketchup (or tomato paste)

1/2 teaspoon garlic powder

1/4 teaspoon salt

1 tablespoon sweetener that measures like sugar

1/2 cup diced carrots

1 small red bell pepper, diced

2 cups snow peas

1 (8-ounce) can water chestnuts, drained, optional

Sesame seeds for garnish

Whole grain rice or quinoa, optional

Cut the chicken into bite-size pieces. Spray a 6-quart slow cooker with cooking spray. Place the chicken in the slow cooker. In a small bowl whisk together the cider vinegar, soy sauce, ketchup, garlic powder, salt, and sweetener and add it to the slow cooker. Cover the slow cooker and cook on low for 5 to 6 hours or on high for 2 to 3 hours, or until the chicken is cooked through and the sauce has thickened. During the last hour of cooking, add in the carrots, bell peppers, snow peas, and water chestnuts, and stir to combine. Remove the chicken and veggies from the slow cooker, sprinkle with sesame seeds, and serve warm with whole grain rice or quinoa if desired.

Yields 4 Servings (1 cup per serving)
Nutritional Information Per Serving: 167 calories; 3 grams fat; 6 grams carbohydrates; 2 grams fiber; 3 grams sugar; 27 grams protein

NOTE: The sauce should be thick after cooking, but if it is still too thin, simply turn the heat to the warm setting and let sit for 30 to 60 additional minutes to let it thicken further.

BARBECUE CHICKEN TWICE-BAKED SWEET POTATOES

🕐 Estimated Time: 35 minutes

2 medium sweet potatoes

1 (15-ounce) can tomato sauce

3 tablespoons prepared mustard

2 tablespoons cider or white vinegar

1 tablespoon honey

1/4 teaspoon salt

1/8 teaspoon black pepper

1/4 teaspoon garlic powder

1/4 teaspoon onion powder

1/2 cup sweetener that measures like sugar

1/2 teaspoon paprika

1 tablespoon Worcestershire sauce

1/2 teaspoon chili powder, optional

1 cup shredded cooked chicken breast

1/3 cup shredded reduced-fat Cheddar cheese

Sliced green onions for garnish, optional

Chives for garnish, optional

The highlight of this dish is the "clean" barbecue sauce. In fact, I created this recipe to revolve around it. Ready in less than 30 minutes and freezer friendly, this is a complete and well-balanced meal that is easy to prepare. These potatoes are incredibly delicious and guaranteed to please even the pickiest of eaters.

Preheat the oven to 450 degrees. Line a rimmed baking sheet with foil and spray with cooking spray. Scrub the sweet potatoes until the skins are clean, and pierce with a knife to allow the steam to release. Microwave the sweet potatoes for 5 to 10 minutes or until tender. Let cool for 5 minutes. Cut in half lengthwise. Scoop the inside of the sweet potato out of the peel, leaving a thin layer of potato inside the peel so that it can stand up on its own. Place the inside of the sweet potatoes into a medium bowl and set aside. Spray the potato skins with cooking spray and bake for 5 to 7 minutes to get the outside slightly crispy.

While the potatoes are cooking, prepare the sauce. In a small saucepan combine the tomato sauce, mustard, vinegar, honey, salt, pepper, garlic powder, onion powder, sweetener, paprika, Worcestershire, and optional chili powder and stir to combine. Bring the sauce to a boil over medium-high heat and reduce the heat to low. Let simmer, stirring frequently for 5 to 10 minutes or until the sauce begins to thicken.

Mash the inside of the sweet potatoes and add the chicken

and 1/2 cup of the sauce. Remove the sweet potato skins from the oven and fill each skin with the sweet potato and chicken mixture. Turn the oven to broil. Pour the rest of the barbecue sauce over the potatoes and sprinkle the cheese evenly over the top of the potatoes. Place the stuffed potatoes under the broiler for 2 to 3 minutes or until the cheese is bubbling and golden. Remove immediately and sprinkle with green onions or chives if desired.

Yields 4 Servings
Nutritional Information Per Serving: 204 calories; 4 grams fat; 25 grams carbohydrates; 4 grams fiber; 8 grams sugar; 17 grams protein

SLOW COOKER HONEY SESAME PORK

🕐 Estimated Time: 45 minutes or 4 to 8 hours

The slow-cooking process in this dish makes for a moist pork tenderloin that is bursting with flavor. This recipe is unbelievably easy, yet it looks and tastes like you spent hours in the kitchen.

1 pound lean pork tenderloin (or boneless, skinless chicken breasts)

1 small onion, diced

2 teaspoons minced garlic

2 tablespoons honey

1/4 cup low-sugar ketchup

1/4 cup reduced-sodium soy sauce

1 1/2 tablespoons sesame seeds, divided

1 (8-ounce) can crushed pineapple, drained

1/4 teaspoon red pepper flakes, optional

1/4 cup water

1 tablespoon cornstarch

1 to 2 green onions, chopped, optional

Whole grain rice, quinoa, or broccoli for serving, optional

Spray a 6-quart slow cooker with cooking spray. Place the pork tenderloin in the slow cooker. In a medium bowl combine the onions, garlic, honey, ketchup, soy sauce, 1 tablespoon sesame seeds, pineapple, and optional red pepper flakes. Pour the sauce over the pork. Cook on high for 4 hours or low for 8 hours. Once the pork is done cooking, remove it to a cutting board. Allow pork to rest for about 5 minutes.

While the pork is cooling, mix the water and cornstarch in a small bowl until the cornstarch is dissolved. Pour the sauce from the slow cooker into a small saucepan. Bring the sauce to a boil over high heat and reduce to medium-low, stirring frequently. Add the cornstarch mixture to the saucepan. Continue to stir until the sauce thickens. Remove the pan from the heat. If desired, steam broccoli (or veggie of choice) or prepare quinoa or rice according to package instructions. Cut the pork into 8 individual portions. (You can also shred the pork if you would like to make a shredded pork version.) Divide cooked broccoli, quinoa, or rice among plates and top with pork. Spoon the sauce over the top and

sprinkle with the remaining $1/2$ tablespoon sesame seeds and chopped green onions if desired.

Yields 8 Servings
Nutritional Information Per Serving: 160 calories; 5 grams fat; 12 grams carbohydrates; 1 gram fiber; 8 grams sugar; 16 grams protein

OPTIONAL COOKING METHOD: Place the pork in a baking or roasting pan, pour the sauce over the pork, and bake at 350 degrees for 30 to 40 minutes or until the pork reaches an internal temperature of at least 155 degrees.

BROCCOLI AND CHEESE STUFFED CHICKEN BREASTS

🕐 Estimated Time: 45 minutes or 2 to 4 hours

1 cup frozen broccoli florets, thawed in the microwave (or 1 head fresh broccoli, trimmed and lightly steamed)

1/4 cup low-fat cottage cheese

1 large egg white

2 tablespoons plus 1/4 cup grated Parmesan cheese, divided

1/2 cup shredded reduced-fat Cheddar cheese

1 teaspoon minced garlic (or 1/2 teaspoon garlic powder)

1 teaspoon dried minced onion (or 1/2 teaspoon onion powder)

Pinch of salt

Pinch of black pepper

4 boneless, skinless chicken breasts

1/4 cup whole wheat Italian bread crumbs (or panko bread crumbs)

Broccoli and Cheese Stuffed Chicken Breasts present beautifully and look like they took hours to prepare. Not to mention, the taste is phenomenal! The only down side is that the average broccoli and cheese stuffed chicken breast has around 300 calories per chicken breast. This recipe is guaranteed to please even the pickiest eater in a much healthier way.

Preheat the oven to 400 degrees. Spray a 9 x 13-inch baking dish with cooking spray. In a large bowl mix together the broccoli, cottage cheese, egg white, 2 tablespoons Parmesan, Cheddar, garlic, onion, and salt and pepper until well combined. Place each chicken breast between plastic wrap or in a large zip-top bag and pound thin using a mallet or rolling pin. Place approximately 1/4 cup of stuffing on each chicken breast and roll the chicken tightly over the stuffing. Secure the chicken breasts with toothpicks.

In a small bowl mix together the bread crumbs and the remaining 1/4 cup Parmesan cheese. Sprinkle the topping over each chicken breast. Place the chicken breasts in the prepared baking dish (if not using toothpicks to secure, place seam side down). Bake uncovered for 30 to 40 minutes, or until the chicken reaches an internal temperature of 165 degrees.

Yields 4 Servings
Nutritional Information Per Serving: 215 calories; 6 grams fat; 3 grams carbohydrates; 1 gram fiber; 0 grams sugar; 36 grams protein

NOTE: You can also make this in a slow cooker. Pour 1/2 cup chicken broth in the slow cooker and put the stuffed chicken breasts in. Cover and cook on low heat for 4 hours or on high heat for approximately 2 hours or until fully cooked (or when chicken reaches an internal temperature of 165 degrees). Enjoy!

SLOW COOKER ITALIAN MEATBALLS

🕐 Estimated Time: 4 or 6 hours

If you are looking for a quick and easy weeknight meal that the whole family will love, this is the recipe for you. These meatballs are moist and packed full of flavor, and the best part is they only take a few moments to prepare. Simply place them in the slow cooker in the morning and you will have a warm and delicious dinner ready when you get home. I love these meatballs with spaghetti squash, but they are also delicious with a side of vegetables or over some high-fiber pasta.

Meatballs

1 pound extra-lean ground turkey (or lean ground beef)

$1/2$ cup old-fashioned oats

1 large egg, beaten

$1/4$ cup grated Parmesan cheese, plus more for serving

1 tablespoon dried parsley (or 2 tablespoons fresh parsley, finely chopped)

1 teaspoon dried basil

1 teaspoon dried oregano

$1/4$ teaspoon salt

$1/4$ teaspoon black pepper

$1/2$ teaspoon garlic powder

Sauce

$1/2$ onion, finely chopped, optional

2 cups fresh spinach, roughly chopped, optional

1 (16-ounce) jar spaghetti sauce (or tomato sauce)*

1 (15-ounce) can diced tomatoes

High-fiber pasta (or 1 large spaghetti squash) for serving

In a large bowl combine the ground turkey, oats, egg, Parmesan, parsley, basil, oregano, salt, pepper, and garlic powder and mix using your hands. Do not overmix. Roll the mixture into balls the size of a golf ball. In a large nonstick skillet on medium-high heat, add the meatballs (without overcrowding) and cook for about 1 minute, until they are slightly browned. If using onions and spinach, place them in the bottom of a 6-quart slow cooker. Place the meatballs on top of the onions and spinach. Pour the sauce and tomatoes evenly over the top, making sure to coat everything with sauce. Cover and cook on low for 5 to 6 hours or on high for 3 to 4 hours. Serve with high-fiber pasta or spaghetti squash. Sprinkle Parmesan over the top right before serving.

Yields 8 Servings (2 meatballs with $1/4$ cup sauce per serving)
Nutritional Information Per Serving: 120 calories; 3 grams fat; 6 grams carbohydrates; 1 gram fiber; 2 grams sugar; 16 grams protein

* I recommend Classico Tomato & Basil spaghetti sauce with 50 calories per $1/2$ cup.

MINI MEATLOAVES

🕐 Estimated Time: 55 minutes

Meatloaves

2 slices light whole grain bread (or 1/2 cup old-fashioned oats or whole grain bread crumbs)

1 1/4 pounds extra-lean ground turkey (or lean ground beef)

1/3 cup finely diced carrots

1/2 cup finely diced red bell pepper

1/4 cup finely diced white onion

1 large egg

1/2 cup low-sugar ketchup

2 tablespoons low-sugar barbecue sauce

1 teaspoon prepared mustard

1/4 teaspoon salt

1/8 teaspoon black pepper

1/2 teaspoon garlic powder

Topping

1/4 cup low-sugar ketchup

1/2 teaspoon prepared mustard

1 tablespoon low-sugar barbecue sauce, optional

Preheat the oven to 375 degrees. Line a 12-cup muffin tin with silicone or foil liners and spray with cooking spray. Place the bread in a food processor and pulse until the bread is the texture of fine crumbs. Transfer the bread crumbs to a medium bowl and mix with the ground meat. Add the diced carrots, bell peppers, and onions to the meat and bread mixture and use your hands to mix well. Add the egg, ketchup, barbecue sauce, mustard, salt, pepper, and garlic powder. Use your hands to combine the mixture thoroughly. Divide the mixture among the 12 muffin cups (or place in a loaf pan for traditional meatloaf).

For the topping, place the ketchup, mustard, and optional barbeque sauce in a small bowl and stir until combined. Brush the mixture over each meatloaf and put the muffin tin in the oven. Cook until a meat thermometer inserted in the center reads 165 degrees or until the meat is no longer pink in the center, 35 to 45 minutes. If the tops become too brown, but the middle is not fully cooked, cover the meatloaves with foil for the remaining cooking time.

When I was growing up I was convinced that my mom was the best cook ever when she made her famous meatloaf. You see, this wasn't any ordinary meatloaf . . . her meatloaf was so good that I requested it for special occasions. I re-created my mother's famous meatloaf into a much healthier version, but with all the same flavors. I also made them mini so they are great for on-the-go meals and are kid friendly. I hope you enjoy this healthy spin on this melt-in-your-mouth meatloaf as much as my family and I do.

Yields 6 Servings (2 meatloaves per serving)
Nutritional Information Per Serving: 180 calories; 8 grams fat; 10 grams carbohydrates; 2 grams fiber; 2 grams sugar; 22 grams protein

MEDITERRANEAN CHICKEN KABOBS WITH QUINOA TABBOULEH

🕐 Estimated Time: 1 hour and 35 minutes

When I go out to eat, one of my favorite places to go is a Mediterranean restaurant. My husband and I always get the chicken kabobs because the flavors are out-of-this-world good! I generally order a side of tabbouleh, which pairs perfectly with the chicken. I re-created this dish at home using no oils, half the sodium, and quinoa to pump up the fiber and protein in the tabbouleh. My husband tried this dish and exclaimed that he would rather eat this from home any day than go out to eat. Now that is a recipe success in my book.

Marinated Chicken

2 tablespoons balsamic vinegar

2 tablespoons red wine vinegar

Juice of 1 lemon (or 3 tablespoons lemon juice)

2 tablespoons minced garlic

1 tablespoon dried oregano

2 teaspoons dried thyme

1 teaspoon salt

1/4 teaspoon black pepper

1 teaspoon sweetener that measures like sugar

1 pound boneless, skinless chicken breasts, cut into pieces (about 4 chicken breasts)

Quinoa Tabbouleh

1 1/2 cups water

1/2 cup quinoa (or whole grain rice)

1/2 cup diced English cucumber (or 1/2 of a regular cucumber with seeds scraped out and diced)

1/2 cup grape tomatoes, halved

1/2 cup finely diced white onion

1/2 cup chopped flat-leaf parsley

1/2 teaspoon salt, or to taste

1/4 teaspoon black pepper, or to taste

1/2 teaspoon minced garlic (or 1/4 teaspoon garlic powder)

Juice of 1 lemon (or 3 tablespoons lemon juice)

To marinate the chicken: In a small bowl mix the balsamic vinegar, red wine vinegar, lemon juice, garlic, oregano, thyme, salt, pepper, and sweetener. Place the chicken breast pieces in a dish and pour the marinade over them, tossing them in the marinade to ensure that they are completely coated. (Or put everything for the marinade in a zip-top bag and add the chicken.) Cover and place in the fridge for at least 1 hour.

To make the tabbouleh, pour the water and quinoa into a small saucepan and bring to a boil over high heat. Cover and reduce the heat to medium-low to simmer until all the water is absorbed, about 10 minutes. Remove the pan from the heat and set aside to let cool. You will know the quinoa is done when the grain appears soft and translucent. (If using whole

grain rice, cook rice according to package directions.) Once the quinoa has cooled, spoon it into a medium bowl and add the cucumber, tomatoes, onions, parsley, salt, pepper, garlic, and lemon juice. Stir to combine.

To prepare the dish, preheat the grill or grill pan to medium-high heat. Place the chicken on skewers and cook, turning the skewers until the meat has reached an internal temperature of 165 degrees or is cooked through (white in the center). (Grill time will vary depending on the size and thickness of the meat.) Remove and serve over tabbouleh.

Yields 4 Servings (4 ounces of chicken with $1/2$ cup quinoa tabbouleh)
Nutritional Information Per Serving: 203 calories; 4 grams fat; 14 grams carbohydrates; 1 gram fiber; 1 gram sugar; 28 grams protein

PESTO PASTA WITH CHICKEN

🕐 Estimated Time: 25 minutes

2 tablespoons water

3 cups packed fresh spinach

1/2 cup grated Parmesan cheese, plus extra for serving

1/4 cup pine nuts (or walnuts)

3 teaspoons minced garlic, divided

1/2 teaspoon salt

6 ounces (2 cups) dry pasta, such as high-fiber mini farfalle (or 1 medium spaghetti squash, prepared)

1 pound boneless, skinless chicken breasts, cut into cubes

Peas for serving, optional

Combine the water, spinach, Parmesan, pine nuts, 2 teaspoons garlic, and salt in a blender or food processor. Process for about 1 minute or until well combined and smooth. Bring a medium pot of water to a boil over high heat. Add the pasta and cook according to package directions, generally 8 to 10 minutes or until pasta is tender. Drain and set aside.

Heat a large skillet with a generous amount of cooking spray over medium. Place the chicken cubes and the remaining 1 tablespoon garlic in the skillet and cook the chicken for 4 to 6 minutes, turning it frequently for even cooking, until the chicken is lightly browned on the outside and there is no pink on the inside. (Note: During this step I usually add about 1/4 to 1/2 cup water a little at a time to the pan to help the chicken cook through and keep it moist.) Turn off the heat and add half of the pesto to the pan, stirring to coat the chicken evenly. Toss the pasta in the rest of the pesto and top with the chicken and additional Parmesan and peas if desired.

Yields 4 Servings (1 cup pasta, 4 ounces chicken, 1/4 cup pesto)
Nutritional Information Per Serving (with pasta): 355 calories; 13 grams fat; 13 grams carbohydrates; 6 grams fiber; 2 grams sugar; 40 grams protein
(with spaghetti squash): 298 calories; 13 grams fat; 12 grams carbohydrates; 3 grams fiber; 4 grams sugar; 34 grams protein

Most pesto recipes call for tons of oil, which isn't necessarily unhealthy, but it certainly does spike the calorie content of the dish. This recipe features a pesto recipe I created using spinach and pine nuts that packs a powerful flavor punch and adds a moderate amount of healthy fats to the dish. This is a wonderful balance of protein, whole grains, and healthy fats. This dish would also be excellent paired with spaghetti squash instead of the pasta.

VARIATION: This dish can be served with spaghetti squash instead of pasta. Pierce the spaghetti squash with a knife to release the steam while cooking. Microwave for 5 to 10 minutes or until soft. Cut the spaghetti squash in half and discard the seeds. Remove 2 packed cups of the "spaghetti" noodles from the squash and blot dry with a kitchen towel to remove excess moisture. Mix the chicken and pesto together and serve on top of squash.

PULLED BARBECUE PORK

🕐 Estimated Time: 4 or 8 hours

This recipe is healthy, quick, and a great family pleaser. The slow-cooking process makes for unbelievably tender barbecue pork that is bursting with flavor. Serve on sandwich thins, whole grain buns, or a lettuce wrap.

1 pound lean pork tenderloin (or 1 pound boneless, skinless chicken breasts)

1/2 onion, finely chopped

2 tablespoons honey

2 tablespoons cider vinegar

1 (15-ounce) can tomato sauce

3 tablespoons prepared mustard

1/4 cup sweetener that measures like sugar

1 teaspoon garlic powder

1/2 teaspoon paprika

1/4 teaspoon salt

1/4 teaspoon onion powder

1/8 teaspoon black pepper

4 sandwich thins (or whole grain buns or lettuce wraps), for serving

Spray a 6-quart slow cooker with cooking spray. Place the pork tenderloin in the slow cooker. In a medium bowl place the chopped onion, honey, cider vinegar, tomato sauce, mustard, sweetener, garlic powder, paprika, salt, onion powder, and pepper. Whisk to combine. Pour the sauce over the pork tenderloin. Cover and cook for 4 hours on high or 8 hours on low. After cooking, remove the pork tenderloin from the slow cooker and shred the meat with two forks. Place the shredded meat back into the slow cooker and toss the meat in the sauce until it is evenly coated. Serve on sandwich thins, whole grain buns, or lettuce wraps if desired.

Yields 4 Servings (1/2 cup per serving)
Nutritional Information Per Serving: 337 calories; 7 grams fat; 40 grams carbohydrates; 7 grams fiber; 14 grams sugar; 28 grams protein

GENERAL TSO SLOW COOKER CHICKEN

🕐 Estimated Time: 4 or 8 hours

1 pound boneless, skinless chicken breasts, cut into cubes

2 tablespoons cornstarch

1/4 cup low-sugar ketchup

3 tablespoons honey

1/4 cup reduced-sodium soy sauce

1/4 to 1/2 teaspoon red pepper flakes (or 1/2 teaspoon paprika)

2 teaspoons minced garlic (or 1 teaspoon garlic powder)

2 tablespoons dried minced onion (or 1 teaspoon onion powder)

1 1/2 teaspoons ground ginger

2 tablespoons sweetener that measures like sugar

1/2 tablespoon sesame seeds

General Tso's chicken is a very popular Chinese take-out food that is typically deep fried and covered in a heavy sauce. This healthier version has a delicious sauce that is slightly sweet and slightly spicy and is easy to make. With this recipe there is never any excuse to order take-out again.

Spray a 6-quart slow cooker with cooking spray. Place the chicken and cornstarch in a bowl and toss the chicken in the cornstarch until it is evenly coated. Place the chicken in the slow cooker. In a small bowl place the ketchup, honey, soy sauce, red pepper flakes, garlic, onion, ginger, and sweetener and whisk to combine. Pour the sauce over the chicken and toss the chicken in the sauce until it is coated. Cover and cook on high for 2 to 4 hours or on low for 6 to 8 hours. (You will know it is ready when the sauce has thickened and the chicken is cooked through.) Sprinkle sesame seeds on top of the chicken and enjoy!

Yields 4 Servings (1/2 cup per serving)
Nutritional Information Per Serving: 209 calories; 3 grams fat; 18 grams carbohydrates; 0 grams fiber; 10 grams sugar; 27 grams protein

SLOW COOKER TURKEY CHILI

🕐 Estimated Time: 4 or 8 hours

When I'm in need of a quick and healthy meal and I don't have hours to spend in the kitchen, I often whip up a batch of slow-cooked chili. Turkey chili is a wonderful slow cooker dish when you want a balanced meal that is warm and filling. This chili is great for kids, as it is pretty mild, and it's bursting with flavor that is sure to please the whole family.

1 pound extra-lean ground turkey

1 onion, chopped

1 teaspoon minced garlic

1 green bell pepper, chopped

1 (15-ounce) can kidney beans, drained and rinsed

1 (15-ounce) can pinto beans, rinsed and drained

1 (15-ounce) can corn, drained

1 (28-ounce) can crushed tomatoes

1 (15-ounce) can petite diced tomatoes

3 tablespoons chili powder, or to taste

1 tablespoon honey

1 teaspoon salt, or to taste

Pinch of black pepper

Spray a large nonstick skillet with cooking spray and place over medium-high heat. Add the ground turkey, onions, and garlic to the skillet and cook, breaking up the turkey until it is cooked through, about 4 to 6 minutes. Add the turkey mixture to a 6-quart slow cooker and add the bell pepper, kidney beans, pinto beans, corn, crushed tomatoes, diced tomatoes, chili powder, honey, salt, and black pepper. Cover and cook on low for 8 hours or on high for 4 hours.

Yields 8 Servings (1 cup per serving)
Nutritional Information Per Serving: 192 calories; 1 gram fat; 26 grams carbohydrates; 7 grams fiber; 4 grams sugar; 20 grams protein

WHITE CHICKEN ENCHILADA BAKE

🕐 Estimated Time: 35 minutes

2 1/2 cups shredded cooked chicken breast

1 cup canned petite-diced tomatoes, drained

3/4 cup plain nonfat Greek yogurt

1 (4-ounce) can chopped green chilies

1 teaspoon taco seasoning

1/2 cup low-fat cottage cheese

1 cup white corn

1 cup white beans (such as great Northern)

6 high-fiber tortillas, cut into quarters

1 cup low-fat shredded mozzarella cheese

2 green onions, chopped

Preheat the oven to 375 degrees. Spray a 9 x 9-inch baking dish with cooking spray. In a medium bowl mix the chicken with the tomatoes, yogurt, green chilies, taco seasoning, cottage cheese, corn, and beans. Place two of the cut tortillas on the bottom of the prepared baking dish, followed by the chicken mixture. Repeat the layers and end with the tortilla layer. Top with the mozzarella. Bake for 25 to 30 minutes or until the cheese is melted. Top with green onions.

Yields 8 Servings
Nutritional Information Per Serving: 252 calories; 8 grams fat; 28 grams carbohydrates; 11 grams fiber; 4 grams sugar; 28 grams protein

This White Chicken Enchilada Bake is guaranteed to be a new dinner favorite. This recipe tastes a lot like an enchilada without all of the time it takes to prepare and roll each enchilada. Your family will never know they are eating healthy when you serve them this creamy and cheesy Mexican dish.

SPAGHETTI SQUASH ALFREDO

◷ Estimated Time: 40 minutes

If you are a lover of all things creamy and cheesy, you will love this Alfredo spaghetti squash recipe. The cheese sauce is packed with protein so you don't even need meat to make it a complete meal. Spaghetti squash is an incredible and delicious swap for pasta, and when you cook it in the microwave it's ready in minutes. So, if you are looking to trade in the pasta, start with this light and healthy spin on Alfredo. I can promise you won't be missing a thing.

1 medium spaghetti squash

3/4 cup low-fat plain Greek yogurt (or low-fat sour cream)

3/4 cup low-fat cottage cheese

3 tablespoons unsweetened almond milk (or low-fat milk)

1 1/4 cups grated Parmesan cheese

1 teaspoon garlic powder

1/8 teaspoon black pepper

1 cup shredded or chopped cooked chicken breast, optional

1/2 cup shredded mozzarella cheese

2 tablespoons grated Parmesan cheese

Parsley, optional garnish

Preheat the oven to 450 degrees. Line a rimmed baking sheet with foil and spray with cooking spray. (A baking dish will work as well.) Pierce the spaghetti squash with a knife to allow the steam to release and microwave for 5 to 10 minutes or until soft. (Or bake the squash in the oven at 350 degrees for 30 to 45 minutes or until squash is soft.) Cut the squash in half and discard the seeds. Use a fork to gently scrape the "spaghetti" strands into the center of each half of the spaghetti squash and place on prepared baking sheet. Combine the yogurt, cottage cheese, almond milk, Parmesan, garlic powder, and pepper in a blender and blend until smooth. Scoop into a small bowl and microwave for 1 minute, stir, and microwave for 1 additional minute or until the sauce is smooth.

Divide the sauce equally into the spaghetti squash halves. Gently toss the spaghetti strands to coat as much as possible with the sauce. If desired, divide the chicken between the two squash bowls. Top with the mozzarella and Parmesan. Cook for 15 to 20 minutes or until the cheese is melted and lightly golden brown. Sprinkle with parsley if desired.

Yields 2 Servings (3 cups per serving)
Nutritional Information Per Serving: 404 calories; 16 grams fat; 28 grams carbohydrates; 4 grams fiber; 12 grams sugar; 40 grams protein

NOTE: If you're in a hurry, you can also place the squash under the broiler of the oven for 2 to 3 minutes or until the cheese is melted, but you have to watch it closely and be very careful not to let it burn!

SIDE DISHES

MEDITERRANEAN CHICKPEA SALAD

🕐 Estimated Time: 10 minutes

1 (15-ounce) can chickpeas, drained and rinsed

2 tablespoons chopped flat-leaf parsley

1/2 cup diced red bell pepper

1/2 cup halved Roma tomato

1/2 cup diced cucumber (I recommend English cucumbers for this recipe)

2 tablespoons finely chopped red onion

1/4 cup crumbled reduced-fat feta cheese

2 tablespoons sliced black olives

1/2 tablespoon lemon juice

1/2 tablespoon red wine vinegar

1 tablespoon plain nonfat Greek yogurt

1/4 teaspoon minced garlic

Pinch of salt, or to taste

Pinch of black pepper, or to taste

Pinch of sweetener that measures like sugar

This salad has all of my favorite Mediterranean flavors packed into one awesome dish. This recipe is extremely versatile. It makes a great side dish or a quick and healthy snack, and it also makes a wonderful salad topper that pairs perfectly with grilled chicken breasts.

Drain and rinse the chickpeas and place in a medium bowl. Add the parsley, bell peppers, tomatoes, cucumbers, onions, feta, and olives. In a shaker or water bottle, add the lemon juice, red wine vinegar, yogurt, garlic, salt, black pepper, and sweetener and shake to mix. Pour the dressing over the chickpea salad and toss to coat with the dressing. Chill in the refrigerator for about an hour or enjoy immediately!

Yields 8 Servings (1/2 cup per serving)
Nutritional Information Per Serving: 64 calories; 2 grams fat; 8 grams carbohydrates; 2 grams fiber; 0 grams sugar; 4 grams protein

TWICE-BAKED SWEET POTATO SKIN

○ Estimated Time: 35 minutes

I love the crispy skin of a twice-baked potato in combination with the creamy sweet inside of a sweet potato. With a few simple tweaks, I recreated a traditional twice-baked potato to make it healthier without losing any of the flavors. In fact, when my friends tried these for the first time they said they would order these from a restaurant any day!

1 medium sweet potato, scrubbed

1/2 cup chopped cauliflower

1/4 cup water

1/4 cup low-fat cottage cheese

Pinch of sweetener that measures like sugar, optional

1/4 teaspoon garlic powder

Pinch of salt

Pinch of black pepper

1/4 cup shredded mozzarella cheese

1 slice center-cut bacon, cooked and crumbled, optional

Preheat the oven to 450 degrees. Pierce the sweet potato with a knife to allow the steam to release. Microwave the sweet potato for 5 minutes or until it is fork-tender (or bake at 350 degrees for 45 to 60 minutes or until fork-tender). Let cool for 5 minutes. Cut in half lengthwise. Spoon the sweet potato out of the peel into a small bowl, leaving a thin layer inside with the peel so that it can stand up on its own. Place the peel on a small rimmed baking sheet.

Place the cauliflower in a microwave-safe dish with the water and cover with plastic wrap. Pierce the plastic wrap with a fork and microwave for 3 to 5 minutes or until tender. Drain the water from the cauliflower and mash the cauliflower until it looks like mashed potatoes. Mix together the cauliflower, cottage cheese, sweetener (if using), garlic powder, salt, and pepper in a medium microwavable bowl. Stir the sweet potato pulp into the cauliflower mixture. Microwave the mixture for 2 minutes and stir until well combined. (Cottage cheese curds will melt in the microwave.)

Spray the potato skins with cooking spray and bake for about 5 minutes to get the outsides slightly crisp. Remove from the oven and fill each skin with the sweet potato mixture. Top with mozzarella. Place back in the oven and bake for an additional 10 to 15 minutes or until the cheese is melted. Serve with the crumbled bacon if desired.

Yields 1 Serving
Nutritional Information (may vary based on size of potato): 267 calories; 6.5 grams fat; 40 grams carbohydrates; 51 grams fiber; 2.5 grams sugar; 15 grams protein

SPAGHETTI SQUASH FRITTERS

🕐 Estimated Time: 30 minutes

1 medium spaghetti squash

2 large egg whites

3 tablespoons grated Parmesan cheese

1/2 teaspoon garlic powder

1/2 teaspoon dried minced onion (or 1/4 teaspoon onion powder)

1/8 teaspoon salt

1/8 teaspoon black pepper

Pierce the spaghetti squash with a knife to allow the steam to release. Microwave the squash for 5 to 10 minutes or until soft (or bake in the oven at 350 degrees for 30 to 45 minutes or until the squash is soft). Let cool for about 10 minutes. Cut the squash in half lengthwise. Scrape out the seeds using a fork and discard the seeds. Scrape out the "spaghetti" and measure out 2 cups of squash (or more if you desire to double the recipe). Place the remaining squash in a container and refrigerate for another meal or snack.

Place a large nonstick skillet sprayed with cooking spray over medium heat. Add the squash and cook for 2 to 4 minutes to get the excess moisture out of the squash. Turn off the heat and let the squash cool for about 2 minutes. (Or you could simply squeeze the excess moisture out of the squash by wringing it dry in a kitchen towel.)

In a medium bowl mix together the egg whites, Parmesan, garlic powder, onion, salt, and pepper. Add the squash to the egg mixture and stir until everything is well combined.

Return the skillet to the stove and heat over medium-low. Spray with cooking spray. Scoop about 1/2 cup of the squash mixture onto the skillet and spread with a fork or spoon to form a circle. Cook each side as you would a pancake until both sides are golden brown, pressing each side with the bottom of a spatula to get any excess moisture out while cooking. (This will help them get crispy on the outside too!) Serve warm.

These Spaghetti Squash Fritters are one of my favorite ways to eat spaghetti squash. I love that I get in my vegetables along with a good source of protein, which makes for an ideal snack, side dish, or even light meal. I don't know of a single fritter recipe out there that doesn't include bread crumbs, but this one doesn't, which means they are gluten-free and 100 percent nutritious. They are also delicious and easy to make. This may just be your new favorite way to eat spaghetti squash.

Yields 4 Servings
Nutritional Information Per Serving: 45 calories; 1 gram fat; 5 grams carbohydrates; 1 gram fiber; 2 grams sugar; 5 grams protein

BAKED MAC AND CHEESE

Estimated Time: 45 minutes

One of my favorite dishes growing up was macaroni and cheese. I created a rich and creamy but much healthier version of this comfort food that will bring you straight back to your childhood. The protein and fiber in this dish will keep you feeling satisfied without all of the empty calories. Plus, it sneaks in some vegetables, but I can promise no one will suspect a thing.

2 cups chopped cauliflower florets

1 cup dry high-fiber elbow macaroni noodles

1 large egg

3/4 cup unsweetened almond milk (or low-fat milk)

1/8 teaspoon dry mustard (or 1/2 teaspoon prepared mustard)

1/4 teaspoon garlic powder

1 cup shredded reduced-fat sharp Cheddar cheese, divided

3 tablespoons grated Parmesan cheese, divided

1/4 cup low-fat cottage cheese (or 1 ounce reduced-fat cream cheese)

Pinch of salt

Pinch of black pepper

2 tablespoons whole wheat bread crumbs, optional

Preheat the oven to 425 degrees. Spray 4 individual baking dishes (or one medium baking dish) with cooking spray. Place the baking dishes on a rimmed baking sheet (for easy removal from the oven). Bring a large pot of salted water to a boil over high heat. Add the cauliflower to the boiling water and cook until very soft, about 10 minutes. Remove the cauliflower, reserving the water, and place cauliflower in a blender or food processor. In the same water add the pasta. Cook the pasta until tender, 6 to 8 minutes. Drain the pasta and set aside.

Return the empty pot to the stovetop and turn the heat down to low. In a small bowl whisk together the egg, almond milk, dry mustard, and garlic powder. Pour the egg mixture, 3/4 cup Cheddar, 2 tablespoons Parmesan, cottage cheese, salt, and pepper into the pot. Over low heat, cook the cheese and egg mixture, whisking constantly, until the cheeses melt and the sauce begins to thicken, 5 to 6 minutes. Remove the pot from the heat.

Place the cheese sauce into the blender or food processor with the cauliflower and blend until smooth. Add the pasta to the sauce and stir. Divide the macaroni and cheese between the baking dishes. Sprinkle the remaining 1/4 cup Cheddar, bread crumbs if desired, and 1 tablespoon Parmesan evenly

over each dish. Bake for 15 minutes or until the bread crumbs and Parmesan become golden brown.

Yields 4 Servings
Nutritional Information Per Serving: 207 calories; 7 grams fat; 14 grams carbohydrates; 5 grams fiber; 4 grams sugar; 26 grams protein

CHEESY BROCCOLI BITES

🕐 Estimated Time: 35 minutes

3 cups frozen broccoli florets, thawed, steamed, and blotted dry (or fresh broccoli, steamed)

2 tablespoons low-fat cottage cheese

1/4 cup grated Parmesan cheese

2 large egg whites

1/8 teaspoon salt

Pinch of black pepper, or to taste

1/2 teaspoon garlic powder

1/2 teaspoon dried minced onion

Pinch of sweetener that measures like sugar, optional

3/4 cup shredded mozzarella cheese for topping, optional

Preheat the oven to 450 degrees. Line a 12-cup muffin tin with silicone or foil muffin liners and spray with cooking spray. Chop the broccoli florets into small pieces (no bigger than the size of a marble). In a large bowl add the broccoli, cottage cheese, Parmesan, egg whites, salt, pepper, garlic powder, onion, and optional sweetener. Stir until everything is well combined. Scoop 2 tablespoons of the broccoli mixture into each muffin cup. Lightly press the broccoli mixture down with your fingers. Sprinkle each bite with mozzarella if desired. Bake for 25 to 30 minutes or until lightly golden brown on top. Remove from the oven and enjoy warm!

Yields 12 Broccoli Bites
Nutritional Information Per Bite: 20 calories; 1 gram fat; 1 gram carbohydrates; 0.7 grams fiber; 0 grams sugar; 3 grams protein

These broccoli bites are salty, cheesy, and almost too good to be true! I can honestly say this is one of the tastiest ways I have created to eat your veggies. These broccoli bites make for a delicious protein- and veggie-packed side, snack, or light meal. Who knows, this may just be your new favorite way to get your vegetables as well.

ZUCCHINI TOTS

🕐 Estimated Time: 35 minutes

If you are looking for a recipe that will get your kids to eat and love their vegetables, look no further. This zucchini tot recipe is the perfect way to use up your summer zucchini, and it is such a simple and delicious recipe that it is something you will look forward to making. Enjoy with low-sugar ketchup, tomato sauce, or even pizza sauce.

2 medium zucchini, grated (about 4 cups grated), squeezed dry

2 tablespoons low-fat cottage cheese

1/2 cup grated Parmesan cheese

1/4 cup reduced-fat Cheddar cheese

2 large egg whites

Pinch of black pepper

1/2 teaspoon garlic powder

1/2 teaspoon dried minced onion

Preheat the oven to 450 degrees. Line a 12-cup muffin tin with silicone or foil liners and spray with cooking spray. In a large bowl place the zucchini, cottage cheese, Parmesan, Cheddar, egg whites, pepper, garlic powder, and dried onion and mix until well combined. Divide the mixture among the muffin cups (about 2 heaping tablespoons per muffin cup). Lightly press the filling down in each cup. Bake for 30 to 35 minutes or until the tops are lightly golden brown and firm to the touch.

Yields 12 Zucchini Tots
Nutritional Information Per Tot: 37 calories; 1 gram fat; 3 grams carbohydrates; 1 gram fiber; 1 gram sugar; 4 grams protein

SKINNY LAYERED PIZZA DIP

🕐 Estimated Time: 35 minutes

1 (8-ounce) package fat-free cream cheese, softened*

1/4 cup low-fat plain Greek yogurt

1/4 cup low-fat cottage cheese (or additional 1/4 cup Greek yogurt)

2 tablespoons finely chopped chives (or green onions)

1/2 teaspoon garlic powder

1 teaspoon Italian seasoning, divided

2 tablespoons grated Parmesan cheese

1 cup pizza sauce

3/4 cup shredded mozzarella cheese

1/4 cup finely chopped green bell pepper (or pizza topping of choice)

2 tablespoons chopped mini turkey pepperonis (or regular-size turkey pepperoni, cut into quarters)

1/4 cup chopped olives, optional

When I think about game-day appetizers, two things come to mind: pizza and nachos. This layered pizza dip is a cross between the two. It can be served with baked chips or veggies of your choice.

Preheat the oven to 350 degrees. Spray a 9-inch pie dish (or a 9 x 9-inch baking pan) with cooking spray. In a medium bowl mix together the cream cheese, yogurt, cottage cheese, chives, garlic powder, 1/2 teaspoon Italian seasoning, and Parmesan for the first layer. Spread the cream cheese mixture in the prepared pie pan. On top of the first layer, spread on the pizza sauce, followed by the mozzarella, bell peppers, pepperonis, and ending with the remaining 1/2 teaspoon Italian seasoning and olives if desired. Bake for 25 to 30 minutes or until the cheese is melted and bubbly.

Yields 12 Servings (1/4 cup per serving)
Nutritional Information Per Serving: 63 calories; 2 grams fat; 4 grams carbohydrates; 1 gram fiber; 1.5 grams sugar; 7 grams protein

* Or 1 cup low-fat cottage cheese, pureed in a blender or food processor until smooth. If using cottage cheese instead, leave out the Parmesan cheese, as it would be too salty.

SKINNY GREEN BEAN CASSEROLE

🕐 Estimated Time: 45 minutes

Green bean casserole is a very traditional dish on holidays. However, despite the fact that the star of this dish is a "lean green bean," the traditional version of this recipe can pack as many as 600 calories and 30 grams of fat into a one-cup serving! Enjoy this healthy version at your next holiday feast and impress your guests with an awesome dish that won't weigh them down.

1 (8-ounce) package mushrooms, thinly sliced (about 1 cup)

1 medium onion, finely chopped

1 teaspoon minced garlic

1/2 cup water

1 (14-ounce) bag frozen whole green beans (or about 4 cups fresh)

1 cup plain nonfat Greek yogurt (or low-fat sour cream)

1 teaspoon cornstarch

1 teaspoon salt

1/2 teaspoon black pepper

1/2 teaspoon sweetener that measures like sugar

1 tablespoon dried minced onion

1/2 cup grated Parmesan cheese

1/2 cup panko bread crumbs

Preheat the oven to 350 degrees. Spray a large baking dish with cooking spray. Spray a large skillet with cooking spray over medium heat. Add the mushrooms, onions, garlic, and water. Cook, stirring occasionally, until the water is completely evaporated. Remove the onions and mushrooms from the skillet and place in a medium bowl.

If using frozen green beans, thaw the green beans in the microwave for 5 to 10 minutes, or until thawed. (If using fresh, snip off the ends and place the beans in a large pot of boiling water for about 5 minutes, or until tender, and drain.) Add the green beans to the bowl with the mushrooms and onions. Let cool to room temperature.

In a small bowl mix together the yogurt, cornstarch, salt, pepper, and sweetener. Add the sauce to the green beans and toss until everything is well coated in the sauce. Spoon into prepared baking dish. Mix together the dried onion, Parmesan, and bread crumbs in a small bowl and sprinkle evenly over the top. Bake uncovered for 35 to 40 minutes or until topping is golden brown. Serve warm.

Yields 6 Servings (1 cup per serving)
Nutritional Information Per Serving: 110 calories; 3 grams fat; 13 grams carbohydrates; 2 grams fiber; 4 grams sugar; 9 grams protein

CREAMY PASTA SALAD

🕐 Estimated Time: 20 minutes

2 1/2 cups dry high-fiber pasta of choice, or 1 large head cauliflower, cut into bite-size pieces

1 large red onion, finely diced

1 cup frozen peas, thawed

1 large yellow bell pepper, diced

2 cups broccoli florets, chopped fine (I prefer mine lightly steamed)

1/2 cup crumbled feta cheese

1 1/4 cups plain nonfat Greek yogurt

1 tablespoon prepared mustard

Juice of 1 lemon (or 2 tablespoons lemon juice)

1/2 tablespoon dried basil

1/2 teaspoon salt

1/8 teaspoon black pepper

1 cup diced cooked chicken breast, optional

3 slices center-cut bacon (or turkey bacon), prepared and crumbled

Everyone loves a good pasta salad during the summer months. This dish is loaded with vegetables, feta cheese, and crumbled bacon. It's topped off with a fresh and creamy dressing. This pasta salad could easily be made into a well-balanced meal by adding chopped cooked chicken, turkey breast, or even some tuna fish.

Bring a large pot of water to a boil. Add salt and pasta and cook 8 to 12 minutes, or according to package directions. Drain and set aside to cool. If using cauliflower, steam the cauliflower until slightly tender, but not too soft or it will fall apart in the pasta salad. In a large bowl combine the cooked pasta or cauliflower, onions, peas, bell peppers, broccoli, and feta.

In a medium bowl whisk together the yogurt, mustard, lemon juice, basil, salt, and black pepper until smooth. Add the dressing to the bowl of pasta and chicken if desired, and toss until everything is well combined. Refrigerate until you're ready to serve. (This dish tastes best when it sits at least a couple of hours or overnight in the refrigerator.) Add the cooked and crumbled bacon right before serving.

Yields 8 Servings (1 cup per serving)
Nutritional Information Per Serving (with Pasta): 195 calories; 4 grams fat; 20 grams carbohydrates; 7 grams fiber; 4 grams sugar; 26 grams protein
(with Cauliflower): 121 calories; 4 grams fat; 14 grams carbohydrates; 5 grams fiber; 3 grams sugar; 10 grams protein

SKINNY GUACAMOLE

⏱ Estimated Time: 5 minutes

This recipe has a secret ingredient: zucchini! It lightens up this generally heavy dip. Try this simple and refreshing way to make a healthier version of your favorite guacamole dip today.

3 medium zucchini, roughly chopped

1 medium ripe avocado (slightly soft to the touch)

1 teaspoon minced garlic (or 1/2 teaspoon garlic powder)

2 tablespoons lemon juice

1 teaspoon salt, or to taste

1 large Roma tomato, finely diced*

1/2 medium red onion, finely diced*

1/4 cup finely chopped cilantro*, plus more for garnish

Baked pita chips, optional

In a food processor or high-speed blender, blend the zucchini, avocado, garlic, lemon juice, and salt together until smooth (or until it reaches the texture you desire). Scoop into a bowl and stir in the tomatoes, onions, and cilantro. Garnish with additional cilantro and serve with baked pita chips if desired.

Yields 10 Servings (1/2 cup per serving)
Nutritional Information Per Serving: 30 calories; 1 gram fat; 4 grams carbohydrates; 2 grams fiber; 1 gram sugar; 1 gram protein

* Substitute 1 cup store-bought fresh pico de gallo for the tomato, red onion, and cilantro if desired.

BARBECUE BAKED BEANS

🕐 Estimated Time: 4 1/2 or 8 1/2 hours

3 slices center-cut bacon or turkey bacon, roughly chopped

1 medium onion, chopped (I use a Vidalia)

1 teaspoon minced garlic (or 1/2 teaspoon garlic powder)

2 (15-ounce) cans great Northern beans (or any white bean), not drained

1 (15-ounce) can tomato sauce

1/4 cup low-sugar ketchup (or tomato paste)

1/4 cup cider or white vinegar

2 tablespoons honey

1 1/2 tablespoons prepared mustard

1/4 cup sweetener that measures like sugar, or to taste

Heat a large skillet over medium heat and add the bacon and onions. Cook for 3 to 5 minutes, until the bacon is cooked and onions are translucent. Add the garlic and cook for an additional 30 seconds, then turn off the heat. Add the bacon, onions, and garlic to a 6-quart slow cooker, along with the beans, tomato sauce, ketchup, cider vinegar, honey, mustard, and sweetener. Whisk well to combine. Cover and cook on high for 4 to 5 hours or on low for 8 to 10 hours, stirring occasionally. After cooking, turn the slow cooker to the warm setting or turn off completely and let sit for 30 minutes, which will help the sauce for the beans thicken even more. Serve warm.

Yields 8 Servings (1/2 cup per serving)
Nutritional Information Per Serving: 155 calories; 1 gram fat; 30 grams carbohydrates; 5 grams fiber; 8 grams protein

My husband loves baked beans, so when we got married I started making them all of the time, but now I've found a much healthier way to prepare them. I improved the recipe each time that I made them, until I had it perfected. Soon all of my family and friends were asking for the recipe. I can promise you that no one will know this is a healthier version.

CHEESY CAULIFLOWER GRATIN

🕐 Estimated Time: 45 minutes

One of my favorite side dishes for Thanksgiving when I was growing up was my aunt's cheesy scalloped potatoes. It was a potato dish with a creamy sauce and golden brown topping that seemed to melt in my mouth. I re-created this wonderful childhood memory of cheesy goodness without all of the grease and starch.

This lightened-up version has a creamy sauce (without any flour or butter) and a crispy topping. My family requests it every Thanksgiving, and also throughout the year. I hope you and your family enjoy it as well!

1 large head cauliflower

2 cups water

1 cup plain nonfat Greek yogurt (or low-fat sour cream or low-fat cottage cheese)

1 cup shredded reduced-fat Cheddar cheese, divided

1/2 cup grated Parmesan cheese, divided

1 teaspoon dried minced onion

1/2 teaspoon prepared mustard

1/2 teaspoon black pepper

1/2 teaspoon salt

1/2 teaspoon garlic powder

1/4 teaspoon sweetener that measures like sugar

Preheat the oven to 375 degrees. Spray a large baking dish with cooking spray. Wash the cauliflower and cut into bite-size pieces. Place the cauliflower in a large pot* and add the water. Cover and bring to a boil over high heat. Reduce the heat to medium and cook for 8 to 10 minutes or until the cauliflower is just starting to get tender. Drain the cauliflower in a colander and place in a large bowl.

Mix the yogurt, 1/2 cup Cheddar, 1/4 cup Parmesan, minced onion, mustard, pepper, salt, garlic powder, and sweetener together in a small bowl. Add the sauce to the cauliflower and stir until well combined. Pour into the prepared baking dish. Sprinkle the remaining 1/2 cup Cheddar and the remaining 1/4 cup Parmesan over the cauliflower. Bake 30 to 35 minutes or until the cheese is melted and the topping is lightly golden brown. Serve warm.

Yields 8 Servings (3/4 cup per serving)
Nutritional Information Per Serving: 108 calories; 5 grams fat; 7 grams carbohydrates; 3 grams fiber; 1 gram sugar; 11 grams protein

*Instead of stovetop cooking, you could also microwave the cauliflower in a large microwave-safe dish in 1 cup of water, covered with plastic wrap poked with a few holes for steaming. Microwave for 8 to 10 minutes or until the cauliflower is just starting to get tender. Drain in a colander and place in a large bowl.

WARM CHEESY SPINACH DIP

🕐 Estimated Time: 30 minutes

1 (10-ounce) bag frozen chopped spinach, thawed and squeezed dry

1/2 small onion, finely chopped

1 teaspoon minced garlic (or 1/2 teaspoon garlic powder)

Pinch of salt

Pinch of black pepper

1/4 cup water

1 (5-ounce) can sliced water chestnuts, diced into small pieces

1 1/4 cups low-fat cottage cheese

1/4 cup plus 2 tablespoons grated Parmesan cheese, divided

2 tablespoons crumbled feta cheese

1/2 cup shredded mozzarella cheese

Pita chips or sliced veggies for serving, optional

Preheat the oven to 375 degrees. Spray a small baking dish (8 x 8 inches or smaller) with cooking spray. In a sauté pan combine the spinach, onions, garlic, salt, and pepper with the water. Cover the pan to steam until the onions are soft, stirring occasionally. Remove the lid and continue to stir and cook until the water is completely evaporated. Add the water chestnuts and stir to combine. Turn off the heat.

Add the cottage cheese, 1/4 cup Parmesan, and feta to the sauté pan. Stir to combine. Pour spinach dip into the prepared baking dish and top with mozzarella and the remaining 2 tablespoons Parmesan. Bake for 15 to 20 minutes, or until the cheese is melted and lightly golden brown on top. Enjoy warm and serve with optional pita chips or vegetables if desired.

Yields 12 Servings (1/4 cup per serving)
Nutritional Information Per Serving: 57 calories; 3 grams fat; 3 grams carbohydrates; 1 gram fiber; 1 gram sugar; 6 grams protein

Most cheesy spinach dips are loaded with mayonnaise, sour cream, and butter. In fact, there is nothing healthy about the average spinach dip, despite the word *spinach* in the title and the lush green color. This dip recipe is always a crowd pleaser wherever I bring it. All of the ingredients are healthy, and it's loaded with protein to keep you satisfied!

SNACKS

PEANUT BUTTER BANANA BREAD

🕐 Estimated Time: 45 minutes

1 1/2 cups old-fashioned oats

1/2 cup protein powder (or additional 1/2 cup oats)

1 ripe banana, mashed (about 1/2 cup mashed)

1/2 cup unsweetened applesauce

1/4 cup plain nonfat Greek yogurt (or 1/4 cup additional applesauce)

4 large egg whites (1/2 cup)

1/3 cup creamy peanut butter (or 1/2 cup peanut flour mixed with 1/4 cup water)

1 cup sweetener that measures like sugar

1 teaspoon baking soda

1 teaspoon baking powder

1/4 teaspoon salt

Preheat the oven to 350 degrees. Spray a loaf pan with cooking spray. In a blender place the oats, protein powder, banana, applesauce, yogurt, egg whites, peanut butter, sweetener, baking soda, baking powder, and salt and blend until the batter is smooth. Pour the batter into the prepared loaf pan and bake for 35 to 40 minutes or until a toothpick inserted in the center comes out clean. Let cool and enjoy!

Yields 10 Slices
Nutritional Information Per Slice (with Peanut Butter): 140 calories; 5 grams fat; 14 grams carbohydrates; 2 grams fiber; 4 grams sugar; 11 grams protein
(with Peanut Flour): 112 calories; 1 gram fat; 12 grams carbohydrates; 2 grams fiber; 3 grams sugar; 14 grams protein

I don't know about you, but I think peanut butter and bananas are one of the best flavor combinations. I remember when I was little I would ask for slices of bananas on my peanut butter sandwiches. This childhood favorite got me thinking about how wonderful peanut butter would taste spread on my banana bread . . . and then it hit me: Why not combine the two in the bread? The result is delicious!

PEANUT BUTTER BROWNIE PROTEIN BARS

🕐 Estimated Time: 30 minutes

When it comes to protein bars, let's be honest . . . it's pretty hard to come by one that is delicious, all natural, and inexpensive. So I decided to make my own version. Not only are they inexpensive and easy to make, but I can say without hesitation that they came out tasting better than any protein bar I've ever bought. These bars have no flour, no added sugar, are high in protein, and low in calories. They help you stay full for quite a while and are sure to keep cravings at bay.

3/4 cup black beans, drained and rinsed

1/4 cup unsweetened applesauce

1/4 cup plain nonfat Greek yogurt (or an additional 1/4 cup applesauce)

1/2 cup protein powder (or 1/2 cup old-fashioned oats)

1/4 cup peanut butter, melted (or 1/4 cup peanut flour mixed with 3 tablespoons water)

1/3 cup unsweetened cocoa powder

4 large egg whites

2 teaspoons baking powder

1/2 teaspoon baking soda

1/2 teaspoon salt

1 1/2 cups sweetener that measures like sugar

1/4 cup chocolate chips, optional

Preheat the oven to 350 degrees. Spray an 8 x 8-inch baking pan with cooking spray. In a blender or a food processor place the black beans, applesauce, yogurt, protein powder, peanut butter, cocoa powder, egg whites, baking powder, baking soda, salt, and sweetener and blend until the batter is smooth. Pour batter into the prepared pan. Stir in the chocolate chips or sprinkle on top if desired. Bake for 20 to 25 minutes or until a toothpick inserted in the center comes out clean. Let cool and cut into 9 even squares.

Yields 9 Bars
Nutritional Information Per Bar (with Peanut Butter): 105 calories; 4 grams fat; 8 grams carbohydrates; 3 grams fiber; 1 gram sugar; 12 grams protein
(with Peanut Flour): 75 calories; 0.5 grams fat; 6 grams carbohydrates; 3 grams fiber; 1 gram sugar; 13 grams protein

NO-BAKE PROTEIN COOKIE DOUGH BALLS

Estimated Time: 40 minutes

2 1/4 cups old-fashioned oats, divided

1 cup vanilla protein powder (or flavor of choice)

1/2 cup peanut butter, softened in the microwave for 20 to 30 seconds

2 tablespoons honey

1 cup sweetener that measures like sugar

1/4 teaspoon salt

1/4 cup mini chocolate chips

1/2 cup cold water

Add 3/4 cup oats to a blender or food processor and grind into a flour-like consistency to make oat flour. In a large bowl mix together the remaining 1 1/2 cups oats, oat flour, protein powder, peanut butter, honey, sweetener, salt, chocolate chips, and water until well combined. Scoop 2 tablespoons of the mixture into your hands and roll into a ball and place on a rimmed baking sheet. Continue with rest of the batter. Place the baking sheet in the freezer for about 30 minutes or until the cookie dough balls are firm. Cookie dough balls can be stored in a sealed container in the fridge for up to one week or in the freezer for up to one month.

Yields 26 Protein Balls (or 8 bars)
Nutritional Information Per Protein Ball: 86 calories*, 4 grams fat; 9 grams carbohydrates; 1 gram fiber; 3.5 grams sugar; 5 grams protein

NOTE: This batter can also be made into no-bake protein bars. Simply press the batter into a 9 x 9-inch baking pan sprayed with cooking spray. Freeze for about 30 minutes and cut into 8 bars. Wrap each bar individually and store in the fridge or freezer.

* If cut into bars, 280 calories per bar; 13 grams fat; 28 grams carbohydrates; 3 grams fiber; 11 grams sugar; 16 grams protein

These cookie dough balls are the perfectly balanced treat or snack. They are whole grain, high in protein, and a good source of fat. Not to mention they are sure to satisfy any sweet craving in a healthy way. They can also be made into bars, which can be individually wrapped. This recipe is my go-to when I know I will have a super busy week and will need a quick and healthy source of protein and energy to get me through the day.

FRENCH TOAST PROTEIN MUFFINS

🕐 Estimated Time: 40 minutes

These French toast protein muffins are some of my favorite protein-packed snacks. They are sweetened with just the right amount of maple and spice to create the most amazing French toast–inspired baked good you may have ever put into your mouth! Not to mention they have just a little more than 50 calories per muffin, and all without any flour, oil, butter, or added sugar.

1/2 cup unsweetened almond milk (or low-fat milk)

1/2 cup unsweetened applesauce

1/2 cup low-sugar or low-sugar maple syrup (or honey or agave nectar)

4 large egg whites

1 teaspoon maple extract

1 3/4 cups old-fashioned oats

1/4 cup protein powder (or 1/4 cup additional oats)

1 cup sweetener that measures like sugar

1/2 teaspoon ground cinnamon

2 teaspoons baking powder

1 1/2 teaspoons baking soda

1/2 teaspoon salt

Preheat the oven to 350 degrees. Line 14 cups in 2 muffin tins with foil or silicone liners and spray with cooking spray. In a blender place the almond milk, applesauce, syrup, egg whites, maple extract, oats, protein power, sweetener, cinnamon, baking powder, baking soda, and salt. Blend until the oats are completely ground and the batter is smooth. Divide the batter evenly among 14 muffin cups. Bake for 30 to 35 minutes or until a toothpick inserted in the center of a muffin comes out clean. Let cool and enjoy!

Yields 14 Muffins
Nutritional Information Per Muffin: 55 calories; 1 gram fat; 9 grams carbohydrates; 1 gram fiber; 1 gram sugar; 4 grams protein

SEVEN-LAYER PROTEIN BARS

🕐 Estimated Time: 40 minutes

1 1/2 cups old-fashioned oats

1/2 cup vanilla or plain protein powder

1 teaspoon baking powder

1/2 teaspoon salt

1 teaspoon ground cinnamon

1 cup sweetener that measures like sugar

1/4 cup unsweetened almond milk (or low-fat milk)

1/4 cup honey (or agave nectar)

2 ripe small bananas, mashed (or 2/3 cup unsweetened applesauce)

1/4 cup peanut butter, melted

2 large egg whites

2 tablespoons chocolate chips (I use mini)

2 tablespoons peanut butter chips (or butterscotch chips)

1/4 cup unsweetened coconut flakes*

Preheat the oven to 350 degrees. Spray a 9 x 9-inch baking pan with cooking spray or line with parchment paper. In a large bowl mix together the oats, protein powder, baking powder, salt, cinnamon, and sweetener. In a medium bowl mix together the almond milk, honey, bananas, peanut butter, and egg whites. Add the milk mixture slowly into the oat mixture and stir until everything is combined. Pour the batter into the prepared pan and sprinkle the chocolate chips, peanut butter chips, and coconut flakes over the batter. Bake for 30 to 35 minutes or until the bars are set. Allow to cool completely and cut into 12 bars. The bars will stay fresh for up to one week in a covered container at room temperature or in the refrigerator or freezer for approximately one month.

Yields 12 Bars
Nutritional Information Per Bar: 160 calories; 5 grams fat; 21 grams carbohydrates; 2 grams fiber; 7 grams sugar; 9 grams protein

* I recommend lightly toasting the coconut first. Simply place the coconut flakes on a sheet pan and toast in the oven at 350 degrees for about 5 minutes or until lightly golden brown.

I am beyond excited to share these Seven-Layer Protein Bars with you. It has been my dream to create a healthy seven-layer bar for years now, but it was quite the challenge to keep the taste of the full fat and sugar version you see in the bakeries and coffee shops. The traditional recipe calls for condensed milk, butter, and tons of sugar, which can be hard to replace without losing the flavor. I made it my goal to think of a healthy yet satisfying version of these tasty bars. It was also my goal to make them into protein bars so they would qualify as a well-balanced snack or dessert. So, without further ado . . . I hope you enjoy these Seven-Layer Protein Bars as much as I do!

ALMOND COCONUT GRANOLA

🕐 Estimated Time: 40 minutes

Unlike traditional granola, this recipe is low in sugar and fat, making it a healthy and delicious treat that you can feel good about enjoying and serving to your family. Serve it with high-protein Greek yogurt and you have yourself a well-balanced and tasty breakfast or snack.

2 1/2 cups old-fashioned oats

2 tablespoons coconut oil (or melted butter*)

1 teaspoon coconut extract

1/2 cup sweetener that measures like sugar

2 tablespoons honey

2 tablespoons egg whites

1 teaspoon baking powder

Pinch of salt

1/2 cup coconut flakes

1/4 cup mini chocolate chips

1/2 cup sliced almonds, optional

1/4 cup white chocolate chips, optional

Preheat the oven to 350 degrees. Line a rimmed baking sheet with foil sprayed with cooking spray or parchment paper. In a medium bowl place the oats, coconut oil, coconut extract, sweetener, honey, egg whites, baking powder, and salt and stir until everything is well combined. Place the granola on the prepared baking sheet and bake for 15 minutes. Remove the sheet from the oven and stir to break the granola apart. Add the coconut flakes. Return the sheet to the oven and bake for another 15 to 20 minutes or until the granola is crispy. Let the granola cool completely and add chocolate chips (and almonds or white chocolate chips if desired). Store in an airtight container for up to 7 days.

Yields 7 Servings (1/2 cup per serving)
Nutritional Information Per Serving: 150 calories; 6 grams fat; 35 grams carbohydrates; 5 grams fiber; 6 grams sugar; 4 grams protein

* I like to use Smart Balance Butter.

TRIPLE CHOCOLATE CHUNK MUFFINS

🕐 Estimated Time: 25 minutes

1 3/4 cups old-fashioned oats

3 large egg whites

3/4 cup unsweetened cocoa powder

1/2 cup unsweetened applesauce

1 teaspoon vanilla extract

1/2 cup plain nonfat Greek yogurt (or plain nonfat yogurt)

1 cup sweetener that measures like sugar

1/2 teaspoon cream of tartar (or 2 teaspoons vinegar)

1 1/2 teaspoons baking powder

1 1/2 teaspoons baking soda

1/4 teaspoon salt

1 cup hot water

1/2 cup semisweet chocolate chips, divided

I can honestly say that these are hands down the best chocolate muffins you'll ever have! They are so moist and chocolaty that you may be able to pass them off as dessert. These muffins have been one of my most popular recipes to date.

Preheat the oven to 350 degrees. Line a 12-cup muffin tin with silicone or foil liners and spray with cooking spray. In a blender or food processor add the oats, egg whites, cocoa powder, applesauce, vanilla, yogurt, sweetener, cream of tartar, baking powder, baking soda, and salt. Add the hot water to the blender and blend until the mixture is smooth. Place the batter in a bowl and gently stir in 1/4 cup chocolate chips.* Scoop the batter into the prepared muffin cups. Cook for 10 minutes. Remove the muffins from the oven and distribute the remaining 1/4 cup chocolate chips on top of the muffins. Place the muffins back into the oven and bake for an additional 5 minutes or until a toothpick inserted in the center of a muffin comes out clean. Cool the muffins before removing from the pan.

Yields 12 Muffins
Nutritional Information Per Muffin: 95 calories; 3 grams fat; 23 grams carbohydrates; 4 grams fiber; 4 grams sugar; 5 grams protein

* You could skip this step by putting all of the chips in the batter and baking the muffins for 12 to 15 minutes straight.

STRAWBERRY SHORTCAKE MUFFINS

🕐 Estimated Time: 30 minutes

I am in *love* with strawberries. On my birthday every year I go strawberry picking. With my overabundance of fresh strawberries, I came up with an amazing recipe that would showcase one of nature's finest foods. The first time I made these muffins my whole house smelled like strawberry shortcake. I could barely wait for them to cool before I tried my first bite. I knew instantly that this recipe was going to be a hit for strawberry lovers everywhere. Enjoy!

2 1/2 cup old-fashioned oats

1 cup plain nonfat Greek yogurt

2 large eggs

1 cup sweetener that measures like sugar

1 1/2 teaspoons baking powder

1/2 teaspoon baking soda

2 cups strawberries, diced, patted dry, divided

Preheat the oven to 400 degrees. Line a 12-cup muffin tin with silicone or foil liners. In a blender or food processor mix together the oats, yogurt, eggs, sweetener, baking powder, and baking soda and blend until smooth. Pour the batter into a medium bowl and stir in 1 1/2 cups strawberries. Divide the batter among the muffin cups and bake for 20 to 25 minutes or until a toothpick inserted in the center of a muffin comes out clean. Divide the remaining 1/2 cup diced strawberries over the top of each muffin.

Yields 12 Muffins
Nutritional Information Per Muffin: 93 calories; 2 grams fat; 23 grams carbohydrates; 4 grams fiber; 2 grams sugar; 5 grams protein

BANANA BREAD FOR ONE

🕐 Estimated Time: 5 minutes or 25 minutes

1/2 small banana, mashed

1 large egg white

2 tablespoons peanut flour (or oat flour* or protein powder)

1 teaspoon sweetener that measures like sugar

1/2 teaspoon baking powder

Pinch of ground cinnamon

Pinch of salt

1 tablespoon chopped walnuts, optional

To make in the microwave: Spray a microwave-safe mug or small bowl with cooking spray. In a small bowl place the banana, egg white, peanut flour, sweetener, baking powder, cinnamon, salt, and walnuts if desired and stir until well combined. Pour the batter into the prepared mug or bowl. Place the mug in the microwave and microwave for 1 minute 30 seconds to 2 minutes, until the bread is set. Turn the mug upside down to release.

To make in the oven: Preheat the oven to 350 degrees. Spray an oven-safe individual baking dish or ramekin with cooking spray. Place the banana, egg white, peanut flour, sweetener, baking powder, cinnamon, salt, and walnuts if desired in a small bowl and stir until well combined. Pour the batter into the prepared baking dish. Bake for 20 to 25 minutes or until the bread is set. When cooled, remove from the baking dish and enjoy!

Yields 1 Serving

Nutritional Information: 117 calories; 2 grams fat; 15 grams carbohydrates; 5 grams fiber; 6 grams sugar; 13 grams protein

* Oat flour is made by grinding old-fashioned oats in a blender or food processor until it reaches a smooth, flour-like texture.

What could be better than banana bread that is low in sugar, carbs, and fat and still tastes phenomenal? Banana bread for one, of course! This individually portioned recipe makes a yummy snack, dessert, or post-workout treat. With only a few simple ingredients, you can make banana bread in the microwave in a matter of minutes or in a baking dish in the oven.

SKINNY PIZZA ROLLS

🕐 Estimated Time: 30 minutes

When I was a kid I remember feeling so hungry when I got home from school. My mom would always have a snack ready for my sisters and me when we walked in the door. It was a special treat when she let us have pizza rolls. Looking back, it was a good thing that she limited them to special treats, because they don't exactly pass as a nutritious snack. I decided to make a healthier version of this childhood snack that's just as much fun to make as it is to eat. At only about 30 calories per pizza roll, you can feel good about serving them to your kids or enjoying them for yourself.

1/2 cup pizza sauce (or pasta sauce)

1/2 cup shredded mozzarella cheese

17 turkey pepperonis

1/3 cup diced cooked chicken breast (or cooked light Italian sausage), optional

2 tablespoons grated Parmesan cheese

1 teaspoon Italian seasoning

1/2 teaspoon garlic powder

Pinch of sweetener

Pinch of black pepper

24 wonton wrappers

Preheat the oven to 450 degrees. Prepare a large rimmed baking sheet with parchment paper or foil coated with cooking spray. Pour the pizza sauce and mozzarella in a medium bowl. Slice the pepperonis into quarters and add them to the sauce mixture. If desired, add chicken or sausage. Stir until combined. Add the Parmesan, Italian seasoning, garlic powder, sweetener, and pepper. Stir again until everything is well combined.

Set the wonton wrappers on the prepared baking sheet. Prepare a small bowl of water and set beside the baking sheet. Use a spoon to scoop about a tablespoon of filling into the center of each wrapper. (You could use a little more or less, just try not to overfill them or the filling will come out the sides when you are baking them.) Wet your finger in the water bowl and trace two of the wonton corners with your wet finger. Fold the wrapper in half to meet the two dry corners with the two wet corners. As you press to seal the two sides together, the water will act like glue to seal the corners shut. Once all the wonton wrappers are filled, give them a light spray with cooking spray. Bake for 10 to 15 minutes or until the tops are lightly golden brown.

Yields 24 Pizza Rolls
Nutritional Information Per Pizza Roll: 38 calories; 1 gram fat; 5 grams carbohydrates; 0 grams fiber; 0 grams sugar; 2 grams protein

CARAMEL APPLE SNACK CAKE

🕐 Estimated Time: 25 minutes

2 cups old-fashioned oats

1 cup sweetener that measures like sugar

1 teaspoon baking powder

1/2 teaspoon baking soda

1/2 teaspoon salt

1 teaspoon ground cinnamon

1/2 teaspoon apple pie spice (or pumpkin pie spice)

1 cup unsweetened applesauce

4 large egg whites

1 large egg

1 1/2 teaspoons caramel extract

1 teaspoon almond extract (or vanilla extract)

1 1/4 cups peeled and finely chopped apple (about 1 large apple)

1/4 cup chopped pecans or walnuts, optional

Light whipped topping,* optional

Preheat the oven to 350 degrees. Spray a 9 x 9-inch square or 9-inch round baking dish with cooking spray. Blend the oats, sweetener, baking powder, baking soda, salt, cinnamon, and apple pie spice in a blender or food processor until the oats are finely ground. In a medium bowl add the unsweetened applesauce, egg whites, egg, caramel extract, and almond extract and stir to combine. Add the oat mixture to the applesauce mixture and mix well. Stir in the chopped apples and nuts if desired. Pour the batter into the prepared pan and bake 18 to 20 minutes or until a toothpick inserted in the center comes out clean. Cut into 9 slices and enjoy with whipped topping if desired!

Yields 9 Servings
Nutritional Information Per Serving: 101 calories; 2 grams fat; 17 grams carbohydrates; 2 grams fiber; 4 grams sugar; 5 grams protein

* I like to use truwhip.

I love this recipe because it can be enjoyed in so many different ways. This cake is great for a snack, for breakfast (yes, it's that healthy), or as dessert! At just about 100 calories per slice, and with no added sugar, butter, or white flour, you can have your cake and eat it, too, with this delicious treat!

SKINNY EASY MAC

🕐 Estimated Time: 15 minutes

Easy Mac wasn't around when I was a kid, but I can imagine that it would have been one of my favorite snacks. It's nice to know that you can prepare mac and cheese without a stove top or oven and it's ready in a matter of minutes. I have taken the simplicity of this novel concept and turned it into a much healthier and satisfying dish. I hope you enjoy!

1/3 cup (dry) high-fiber elbow macaroni noodles

1/2 cup water

Pinch of salt

3 tablespoons reduced-fat shredded Cheddar cheese, divided

2 tablespoons unsweetened almond milk (or lowfat milk)

2 tablespoons low-fat cottage cheese

Pinch of black pepper, optional

Pinch of dry mustard, optional

Combine the pasta noodles, water, and salt in a large 4-cup microwave-safe bowl. Microwave for 6 minutes, taking the bowl out and stirring every 2 minutes. (The water should be almost completely absorbed at this point and the pasta should be al dente.) Add 2 tablespoons Cheddar, almond milk, cottage cheese, pepper if desired, and mustard powder if desired. Stir and microwave another 2 minutes or until the cheese and cottage cheese are melted. Stir once more after removing the bowl from the microwave. Add the remaining tablespoon of cheese and stir until everything is combined.

Yields 1 Serving
Nutritional Information: 190 calories; 5 grams fat; 26 grams carbohydrates; 3 grams fiber; 1 gram sugar; 13 grams protein

NO-BAKE PROTEIN BARS

🕐 Estimated Time: 35 minutes

1 1/4 cups old-fashioned oats

3/4 cup raw almonds

1/4 cup protein powder

2 tablespoons unsweetened cocoa powder

1/4 teaspoon salt

1 cup sweetener that measures like sugar

2 tablespoons honey

1/4 cup peanut butter, melted

1/4 cup water

Place the oats and almonds in a blender and blend until they are ground into a flour-like consistency. Pour into a large bowl. Add the protein powder, cocoa powder, salt, and sweetener and mix thoroughly. Add the honey, peanut butter, and water and stir to combine.

Spray a 9 x 5-inch loaf pan with cooking spray. Press the dough evenly into the pan. Place the loaf pan in the freezer for 30 minutes and then cut the dough into 6 bars. Wrap each bar individually in plastic wrap. Store bars in the refrigerator for one week or in the freezer for one month.

Yields 6 Bars
Nutritional Information Per Bar: 220 calories; 11 grams fat; 22 grams carbohydrates; 4 grams fiber; 7 grams sugar; 11 grams protein

If you have ever had a store-bought protein bar, then chances are you discovered that it can be hard to find a bar that has a good taste and good nutrition. These homemade protein bars are easy to make, and they taste as good as they are for you!

LEMON POPPY SEED MUFFINS

⏱ Estimated Time: 35 minutes

If you love lemon poppy seed cake or muffins, this recipe will be right up your alley. The bright flavor of freshly squeezed lemon juice shines in these moist muffins!

1 cup old-fashioned oats

1 cup sweetener that measures like sugar

1/2 cup protein powder (or an additional 1/2 cup oats)

4 large egg whites (1/2 cup)

3/4 cup unsweetened applesauce

2 tablespoons low-fat milk

Juice of 1 lemon (or 2 tablespoons lemon juice)

Zest of 1 lemon (or an additional 2 tablespoons lemon juice)

1 tablespoon poppy seeds

1 teaspoon baking powder

1/2 teaspoon baking soda

Pinch of salt

Preheat the oven to 350 degrees. Line a 12-cup muffin tin with foil or silicone muffin liners and spray with cooking spray. In a blender or food processor place the oats, sweetener, protein powder, egg whites, applesauce, milk, lemon juice, lemon zest, poppy seeds, baking powder, baking soda, and salt and blend until the oats are ground and a smooth batter forms. Divide the batter evenly between the muffin cups. Bake for 25 to 28 minutes or until the muffins are lightly golden brown on top and a toothpick inserted in the center of a muffin comes out clean. Remove from the oven and enjoy! Store in the refrigerator for one week.

Yields 12 Muffins
Nutritional Information Per Muffin: 60 calories; 1 gram fat; 6 grams carbohydrates; 1 gram fiber; 2 grams sugar; 7 grams protein

DESSERT

BLUEBERRY COBBLER FOR ONE IN MINUTES

🕐 Estimated Time: 5 minutes

1/2 cup blueberries

7 tablespoons old-fashioned oats

2 tablespoons unsweetened almond milk (or low-fat milk)

1 tablespoon plain nonfat Greek yogurt (or unsweetened applesauce)

1 to 2 tablespoons sweetener that measures like sugar

1/2 teaspoon baking powder

Pinch of salt

Spray a small microwave-safe bowl or ramekin with cooking spray. Place the blueberries in the bowl or ramekin and lightly press with a fork to smash just a few of the berries. Put the oats in a blender or food processor and grind into a flour-like consistency. Pour the oat flour into a separate small bowl and add the almond milk, yogurt, sweetener, baking powder, and salt. Pour the batter over the berries. Microwave for 1 minute or until the topping is slightly firm to the touch. (It will resemble the texture of a muffin.) Serve warm.

Yields 1 Serving
Nutritional Information: 120 calories; 1.5 grams fat; 24 grams carbohydrates; 8 grams sugar; 4 grams fiber; 3 grams protein

This blueberry cobbler is an excellent way to pack all of the best flavors of summer into a sweet treat. What's even better is that it is ready in minutes, and it is perfectly portioned. You can also try this cobbler recipe with any summer berry or fresh fruit of your choice.

SKINNY DESSERT PIZZA

🕐 Estimated Time: 35 minutes

What could be better than pizza for dessert? This dessert pizza starts with a soft cookie crust that is topped with whipped cream cheese and finished off with a swirl of sweet summer berries. The berries can be swapped out with any fruit. This recipe is guaranteed to be a crowd pleaser at any gathering.

Crust

1/2 cup raw almonds

1 cup old-fashioned oats

1 cup sweetener that measures like sugar

1/4 teaspoon baking soda

1 teaspoon baking powder

1/4 teaspoon salt

1 large egg

2 large egg whites

1/2 cup plain nonfat Greek yogurt

1/2 cup unsweetened almond milk (or low-fat milk)

1/2 teaspoon almond extract (or vanilla extract)

Filling

1 (8-ounce) package fat-free (or low-fat) cream cheese, softened

1/2 cup sweetener that measures like sugar

1 teaspoon vanilla extract

1/2 teaspoon lemon juice

1/4 teaspoon almond extract (or additional vanilla extract)

Topping

1 cup halved strawberries

1/2 cup raspberries

1/2 cup blueberries

To make the crust, preheat the oven to 375 degrees. Spray an 8-inch springform pan with cooking spray. Place the almonds and oats in a blender and blend to a flour-like consistency. Add the sweetener, baking soda, baking powder, salt, egg, egg whites, yogurt, almond milk, and almond extract to the blender and blend until smooth. Pour the mixture into the springform pan and bake for 20 to 25 minutes or until the crust is lightly browned. Cool completely.

To make the filling, beat the cream cheese and sweetener in a medium bowl using a handheld electric mixer. Add the vanilla, lemon juice, and almond extract and lightly beat. Chill the filling in the refrigerator until the crust has cooled completely. Spread the cream cheese mixture over the cooled crust.

To serve, arrange the strawberries, raspberries, and blueberries over the top. Cut the pizza into 8 slices and enjoy!

Yields 8 Servings
Nutritional Information Per Serving: 102 calories; 5 grams fat; 7 grams carbohydrates; 2 grams fiber; 3 grams sugar; 8 grams protein

SOFT-BAKED CHOCOLATE CHIP COOKIES

🕐 Estimated Time: 15 minutes

2 cups old-fashioned oats

1/2 cup protein powder (or an additional 1/4 cup oats)

1 cup sweetener that measures like sugar

1 teaspoon baking powder

1/2 teaspoon baking soda

1/2 teaspoon salt

1 cup unsweetened applesauce

1 cup plain nonfat Greek yogurt

1 (16-ounce) can garbanzo beans, drained and rinsed

1 large egg

1 teaspoon vanilla extract

1/4 cup dark chocolate chips

Soft, chocolaty, and gooey! That pretty much sums up the taste of these cookies. Not to mention they are packed with protein and fiber. These cookies are so good that it may become your new favorite cookie recipe. As an added bonus, they are made with a secret ingredient that pumps up the nutrition factor.

Preheat the oven to 400 degrees. Line a baking sheet with parchment paper or foil and spray with cooking spray. In a blender or food processor place the oats, protein powder, sweetener, baking powder, baking soda, and salt and blend until the oats are completely smooth. Pour into a large bowl and set aside.

Add the applesauce, yogurt, garbanzo beans, egg, and vanilla to the blender or food processor and blend until the beans are ground and smooth. (You may need to scrape mixture down with a spatula to incorporate everything evenly.) Add the applesauce mixture to the oat mixture. Stir in the chocolate chips. Scoop 2 tablespoons of the dough onto the prepared baking sheet and smooth the dough to a disk shape. (I used the back of a spoon to do this.) Repeat with the remaining dough. Bake for 8 to 10 minutes or until just set. Remove from the oven. Let cool completely before serving.

Yields 24 Cookies
Nutritional Information Per Cookie: 68 calories; 1 gram fat; 10 grams carbohydrates; 1 gram fiber; 2 grams sugar; 5 grams protein

BIRTHDAY CAKE PROTEIN CUPCAKES

🕐 Estimated Time: 25 minutes

This recipe is a healthy spin on a very popular birthday cake mix. These cupcakes are so healthy that you could actually eat them for breakfast! They are only about 70 calories, packed with 7 grams of protein, and have no added sugar, flour, or butter. They are also easy to whip up and are a great way to celebrate a birthday or bring some fun to any day of the week.

1 1/2 cups old-fashioned oats

1/2 cup plain or vanilla protein powder (or an additional 1/2 cup oats)

1/2 cup unsweetened applesauce

1/2 cup plain nonfat Greek yogurt

3 large egg whites

1/4 cup unsweetened almond milk (or low-fat milk)

1 teaspoon almond extract

1 teaspoon butter extract (or vanilla extract)

1 cup sweetener that measures like sugar

2 teaspoons baking powder

1/2 teaspoon baking soda

1/2 teaspoon salt

2 tablespoons rainbow sprinkles, plus more for garnish

1 (8-ounce) container light whipped topping*, optional

Preheat the oven to 375 degrees. Line a 12-cup muffin tin with silicone or foil muffin liners and spray with cooking spray. In a blender or food processor place the oats, protein powder, applesauce, yogurt, egg whites, almond milk, almond extract, butter extract, sweetener, baking powder, baking soda, and salt and blend until the batter is completely smooth. Stir in the sprinkles. Pour the mixture into the muffin cups. Bake 18 to 20 minutes or until a toothpick inserted into the center of a cupcake comes out clean. Let cool completely and top with whipped topping and additional sprinkles if desired. (Be sure to wait until they are ready to serve to top with whipped topping.) Leftovers should be stored in the refrigerator.

Yields 12 Cupcakes
Nutritional Information Per Cupcake: 71 calories per serving; 1 gram fat; 9 grams carbohydrates; 1 gram fiber; 2 grams sugar; 7 grams protein

* I recommend truwhip or Light Cool Whip.

BROWNIE FOR ONE IN MINUTES

⏱ Estimated Time: 5 minutes

6 tablespoons old-fashioned oats

3 tablespoons plain nonfat Greek yogurt

2 tablespoons unsweetened almond milk (or lowfat milk)

1 1/2 tablespoons unsweetened cocoa powder

1 1/2 tablespoons sweetener that measures like sugar

1/2 teaspoon baking powder

Pinch of salt

Spray a microwave-safe mug or small bowl with cooking spray. Add the oats to a blender or food processor and grind into a flour-like consistency to make oat flour. Place the oat flour, yogurt, almond milk, cocoa powder, sweetener, baking powder, and salt in a small bowl and stir until well combined. Pour the batter into the prepared mug. Place the mug in the microwave and cook for 1 minute to 1 minute and 30 seconds, depending on how gooey you like your brownie. (You can microwave it for more or less time since there is no egg in it.)

Yields 1 Serving
Nutritional Information: 95 calories; 2 grams fat; 15 grams carbohydrates; 2 grams fiber; 2 grams sugar; 8 grams protein

This is the ideal treat if you are craving something full of chocolate. The best part about this recipe is that it only takes minutes to prepare. Let's face it, we all have those moments when we need chocolate now!

SINGLE-SERVE CHOCOLATE CAKE

🕐 Estimated Time: 5 minutes

This chocolate cake recipe is out of this world and it's ready in minutes!

2 tablespoons peanut flour (or oat flour*)

2 tablespoons plain nonfat Greek yogurt

1 1/2 tablespoons unsweetened cocoa powder

2 large egg whites

1 teaspoon baking powder

1 to 2 tablespoons sweetener that measures like sugar, or to taste

Pinch of salt

Spray a microwave-safe small bowl or mug with cooking spray. In another small bowl place the peanut flour, yogurt, cocoa powder, egg whites, baking powder, sweetener, and salt and stir until well combined. Pour the batter into the prepared bowl. Place in the microwave and microwave for 1 minute 30 seconds to 2 minutes or until cake is set.

Yields 1 Serving
Nutritional Information: 129 calories; 1.5 grams fat; 7 grams carbohydrates; 4 grams fiber; 2 grams sugar; 26 grams protein

OPTIONAL "MOLTEN LAVA" VARIATION: To make it a molten lava cake, place 1 square dark chocolate in the middle of the batter before placing in the microwave.

* Oat flour is made by grinding old-fashioned oats in a blender or food processor until it reaches a smooth, flour-like consistency.

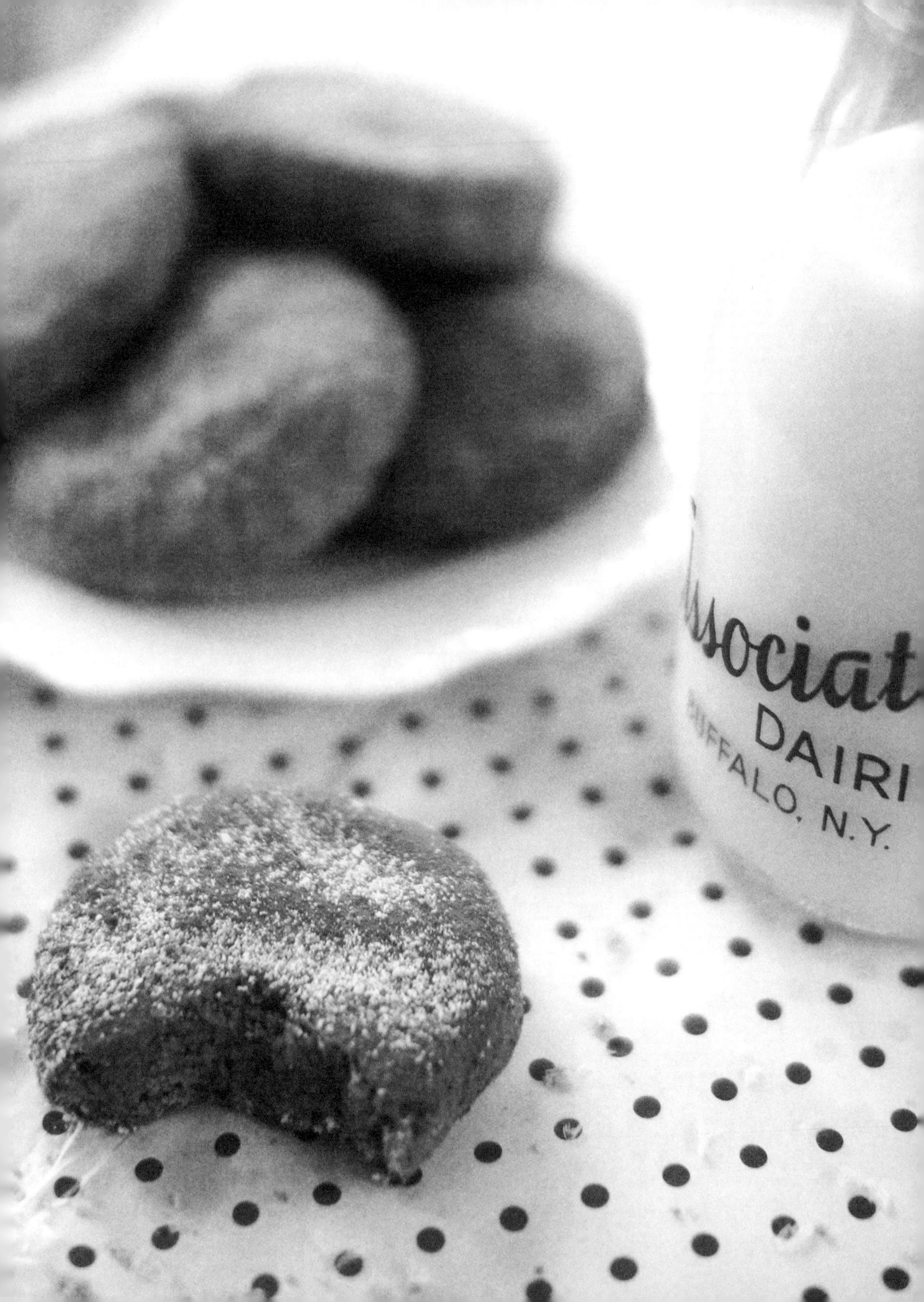
ssociat
DAIRI
FFALO, N.Y.

SOFT-BAKED GINGER DOODLES

⏱ Estimated Time: 15 minutes

1 1/4 cups old-fashioned oats

1 cup raw almonds

1 1/2 cups sweetener that measures like sugar, divided

2 teaspoons ground cinnamon, divided

1 1/2 teaspoons ground ginger

1/4 teaspoon salt

1/4 teaspoon baking soda

1/8 teaspoon pumpkin pie spice

1/2 cup unsweetened applesauce

Preheat the oven to 350 degrees. Line a baking sheet with parchment paper or foil sprayed with cooking spray. In a blender or food processor grind the oats and almonds into a flour-like consistency. Pour into a medium bowl and add 1 cup sweetener, 1 teaspoon cinnamon, ginger, salt, baking soda, and pumpkin pie spice and stir to combine. Add the applesauce and stir until the mixture forms into dough.

In a small bowl combine the remaining 1/2 cup sweetener and 1 teaspoon cinnamon and stir to combine. Scoop 2 tablespoons of the dough and roll into a ball. Flatten the ball between your hands and coat in the cinnamon mixture. Repeat with the remaining dough. Place the cookies on the prepared baking sheet and bake for 8 to 10 minutes. Let cool and enjoy!

Yields 10 Cookies
Nutritional Information Per Cookie: 100 calories; 5 grams fat; 11 grams carbohydrates; 2 grams fiber; 1 gram sugar; 4 grams protein

If you are a fan of a soft cookie with a hint of spice, these cookies are for you! These cookies are essentially a cross between a gingersnap and a snickerdoodle, which creates a wonderful blend of flavors together all in one delicious cookie.

STRAWBERRY PRETZEL DESSERT

🕐 Estimated Time: 2 hours

Strawberry pretzel dessert has been at summer potlucks, parties, and get-togethers for as long as I can remember. So I thought, *Why not make a healthy version that is swimsuit friendly?* This dessert is guaranteed to please, as it has the perfect combination of flavors: a little sweet, a little salty, and don't forget that dreamy whipped cream layer that knocks it out of the park! As an added bonus, it presents beautifully every time.

Strawberry Layer

3 1/2 cups halved strawberries, divided

1/2 cup water

2 tablespoons sweetener that measures like sugar

1 tablespoon unflavored gelatin (or 1 packet Knox gelatin)

2 to 5 drops red food coloring, optional

Crust

1 1/4 cups raw almonds (or 1 cup almond meal)

3 cups pretzel sticks

1/2 cup unsweetened applesauce

1/2 cup sweetener that measures like sugar

1/4 teaspoon salt

Whipped Cream Layer

1/2 cup low-fat cottage cheese

1/3 cup plain nonfat Greek yogurt

1 teaspoon vanilla extract

1 cup sweetener that measures like sugar

1 (8-ounce) container light whipped topping*

Preheat the oven to 400 degrees. Spray an 8 x 8-inch baking pan with cooking spray.

To make the strawberry layer: In a small saucepan combine 2 cups strawberries, water, sweetener, and gelatin and bring to a boil over high heat. Reduce the heat to low and simmer for 3 to 5 minutes or until the berries are soft enough to mash. Mash the strawberries with a whisk while cooking and turn off the heat once the strawberries are mashed and the gelatin is dissolved. Let the gelatin layer cool to room temperature. Chop the remaining 1 1/2 cups strawberries into a fine chop and add to the gelatin mixture along with the food coloring if desired. Refrigerate while preparing the rest of the dish.

To make the crust: Combine the almonds, pretzels, applesauce, sweetener, and salt in a food processor or blender and pulse until the almonds and pretzels are roughly chopped (or place in a zip-top bag and crush with a rolling pin). Press the crust into the prepared baking pan. Bake in preheated oven for 8 minutes. Cool to room temperature.

To make the whipped cream layer: Blend the cottage cheese, yogurt, vanilla, and sweetener in a blender until smooth. Pour into a large bowl and fold in the whipped topping.

To assemble: Pour the whipped cream layer over the cooled crust and spread evenly with a spatula. Pour the gelatin layer over the whipped cream layer and refrigerate at least 2 hours. Once the gelatin layer is set, cut the dessert into 12 squares and serve. Store leftovers in the refrigerator (if you should be so lucky as to have any!).

Yields 12 Servings
Nutritional Information Per Serving: 162 calories; 7 grams fat; 22 grams carbohydrates; 3 grams fiber; 6 grams sugar; 5 grams protein

* I like to use truwhip or Light Cool Whip.

CARROT CAKE FOR ONE IN MINUTES

🕐 Estimated Time: 5 minutes

Cake

1/4 cup finely grated carrots

1 large egg white

2 tablespoons carrot baby food
(or unsweetened applesauce)

2 tablespoons oat flour*

1 teaspoon baking powder

1/4 teaspoon ground cinnamon

Pinch of ground nutmeg

Pinch of salt

1 tablespoon sweetener that
measures like sugar, or to taste

1 tablespoon chopped walnuts,
optional

Optional Frosting

1/4 cup plain nonfat Greek yogurt
(or 1 ounce low-fat cream cheese,
softened in the microwave)

1 tablespoon low-sugar or low-
sugar maple syrup

Dash of ground cinnamon, or to
taste

Dash of stevia, or to taste

What could be better than carrot cake that is portioned out for one serving? Only one thing: the fact that this cake is ready in just a few minutes! At 100 calories per cake, you can truly have your carrot cake and eat it too!

To make the cake, spray a microwave-safe bowl or mug with cooking spray. Place the carrots, egg white, baby food, oat flour, baking powder, cinnamon, nutmeg, salt, sweetener, and walnuts if desired in a small bowl and stir until well combined. Scoop the batter into the prepared mug. Place the bowl in the microwave and cook for 1 minute 30 seconds to 2 minutes or until the cake is set. Turn the bowl upside down to release the cake.

To make the frosting, mix the yogurt with the syrup, cinnamon, and sweetener. Swirl the frosting onto the carrot cake and enjoy!

Yields 1 Serving
Nutritional Information: 100 calories; 1 gram fat; 10 grams carbohydrates; 1 gram fiber; 1 gram sugar; 7 grams protein

*Oat flour is made by grinding old-fashioned oats in a blender or food processor until it reaches a smooth, flour-like texture.

PEANUT BUTTER SWIRL BROWNIES

🕐 Estimated Time: 30 minutes

No, you are not imagining things. This brownie recipe seems too good to be true, but I'm telling you, it's everything it appears to be and more! After replacing the sugar and flour with healthy alternatives, these brownies are just about as good for you as your morning bowl of oatmeal. They are swirled with a thick layer of creamy peanut butter, which makes them simply irresistible. And with just over 100 calories per brownie, they are sure to please both the chocolate and peanut butter fans!

3/4 cup old-fashioned oats

1/2 cup unsweetened cocoa powder

1 cup sweetener that measures like sugar

1 teaspoon baking powder

1/4 teaspoon salt

3/4 cup plain nonfat Greek yogurt

1/4 cup unsweetened almond milk (or low-fat milk)

2 large egg whites

1/2 cup creamy peanut butter

Preheat the oven to 350 degrees. Spray an 8 x 8-inch baking pan with cooking spray. Place the oats, cocoa powder, sweetener, baking powder, and salt in a blender. Blend until the mixture is smooth and the oats are ground up. In a medium bowl combine the yogurt, almond milk, and egg whites. Add the oat mixture and stir until well combined. Pour into the prepared baking pan.

Microwave the peanut butter for 30 seconds. Drizzle the melted peanut butter over the brownie batter. Using a knife, gently swirl the batters together to make a marbled effect. (Be careful not to overmix.) Bake for 22 to 25 minutes or until the brownies begin to pull away from the sides of the pan. Let cool completely and cut into 9 squares.

Yields 9 Servings
Nutritional Information Per Serving: 130 calories; 9 grams fat; 13 grams carbohydrates; 3 grams fiber; 2 grams sugar; 7 grams protein

RICH CHOCOLATE CAKE WITH CHOCOLATE PROTEIN FROSTING

🕐 Estimated Time: 45 minutes

Frosting

1 cup low-fat cottage cheese

1/4 cup unsweetened cocoa powder

1/4 cup sweetener that measures like sugar, or to taste

2 tablespoons sugar-free instant chocolate pudding mix, optional

1 small tub light whipped topping, optional

Cake

3 large egg whites

2 cups sweetener that measures like sugar

1 3/4 cups old-fashioned oats

1 cup low-fat plain Greek yogurt

1 cup unsweetened almond milk (or low-fat milk)

3/4 cup unsweetened cocoa powder

1/2 teaspoon cream of tartar (or 2 teaspoons vinegar)

1 1/2 teaspoons baking powder

1 1/2 teaspoons baking soda

1/4 teaspoon salt

Fresh strawberries or raspberries for topping

What if I told you that you could have a piece of chocolate cake that was low sugar, flour-free, and gluten-free at only 120 calories per serving? This cake tastes so good that my dad (the greatest chocoholic I've ever known) requested it for his next birthday cake! I have to admit that I actually danced in the kitchen when I created this recipe, and I simply couldn't wait to share it with all of you. Be sure to make it for someone you love.

To make the frosting, place the cottage cheese, cocoa powder, and sweetener in a food processor or blender. Process for about 2 minutes until the frosting is creamy and fluffy. Add the pudding mix and fold in the whipped cream with a spatula at this point if desired. Place the frosting in the refrigerator while the cake is baking and cooling.

To make the cake, preheat the oven to 350 degrees. Spray a 9 x 9-inch baking pan or an 8-inch round cake pan with nonstick spray. Place the egg whites, sweetener, oats, yogurt, milk, cocoa powder, cream of tartar, baking powder, baking soda, and salt in a blender or food processor and blend until the oats are ground and the batter is smooth. Pour the batter into the prepared pan and bake for 20 to 25 minutes (9 x 9-inch pan) or 25 to 30 minutes (8-inch round cake pan), or until a toothpick inserted in the center comes out clean. Allow the cake to cool completely before frosting.

Top with sliced strawberries or raspberries if desired. Store leftovers in the refrigerator.

Yields 9 Servings
Nutritional Information Per Serving (with frosting): 120 calories*; 3 grams fat; 27 grams carbohydrates; 7 grams fiber; 2 grams sugar; 11 grams protein

* Without frosting the serving will have 98 calories

GIANT CHOCOLATE CHIP PEANUT BUTTER COOKIE

🕐 Estimated Time: 35 minutes

What could be better than peanut butter cookies? How about one giant peanut butter cookie? This giant cookie has all of the goodness of cookies without all of the time and work that goes into making them.

1/2 cup peanut flour plus 1/4 cup water (or 1/2 cup creamy peanut butter, melted)

1 (15-ounce) can chickpeas, drained and rinsed

1/8 cup sugar-free maple syrup (or honey)

2 egg whites

1/2 cup sweetener that measures like sugar

1 teaspoon baking powder

1/2 teaspoon baking soda

1/2 teaspoon salt

1/4 cup chocolate chips

Preheat the oven to 350 degrees. Spray an 8 x 8-inch baking pan with nonstick cooking spray. Place the peanut flour mixture, chickpeas, syrup, egg whites, sweetener, baking powder, baking soda, and salt in a blender or food processor and blend until the mixture is smooth. Spread the cookie dough on the prepared pan and bake for 30 to 35 minutes or until a toothpick comes out clean and the cookie is set.

Yields 8 Servings
Nutritional Information per serving: 106 calories; 4 grams fat; 13 grams carbohydrates; 3 grams fiber; 5 grams sugar; 7 grams protein

PEANUT BUTTER PROTEIN COOKIES

🕐 Estimated Time: 20 minutes

1 cup peanut butter

1 large egg

1 large egg white

2 tablespoons unsweetened applesauce

1/4 cup vanilla protein powder

1 cup old-fashioned oats

1 cup sweetener that measures like sugar

1 teaspoon baking soda

1/8 teaspoon salt

2 tablespoons mini chocolate chips, optional

These cookies are out of this world! The best part is they have a great balance of healthy fat, protein, and complex carbohydrates, which makes them the perfect treat, snack, or even a quick protein-packed breakfast.

Preheat the oven to 350 degrees. Line a baking sheet with foil sprayed with cooking spray or parchment paper. Place the peanut butter in a microwave-safe bowl and microwave for 30 seconds or until softened and let cool slightly. In a medium bowl mix together the peanut butter, egg, egg white, and applesauce and stir until smooth. In a separate medium bowl mix together the protein powder, oats, sweetener, baking soda, and salt. Add the protein powder mixture to the peanut butter mixture and stir to combine. Stir in the chocolate chips if desired. Moisten your hands (to prevent from sticking) and roll the cookie dough into tablespoon-sized balls. Use a fork to press a crisscross into each cookie. Bake for 8 to 10 minutes. Let cookies cool and serve.

Yields 24 Cookies
Nutritional Information Per Cookie: 85 calories; 6 grams fat; 7 grams carbohydrates; 1.5 grams fiber; 0.5 grams sugar; 7 grams protein

ACKNOWLEDGMENTS

From the bottom of my heart I want to thank:

My heavenly Father. Thank you for taking the broken places of my life and making something beautiful. Everything I have is from you, and it is my greatest desire to use every gift and talent you have given me to bring glory to your name!

My wonderful husband and the creative director and designer of the website Dashing Dish, Sean. You, my sweetie, have encouraged me to follow my heart and follow the Lord's leading, even when it seemed bigger than me. You are the reason I started Dashing Dish. I can honestly say that without you and the Lord, none of this would be possible. Thank you for being my partner in this ministry and in life. You are my best friend and the reason I wake up with a smile in my heart every day.

My two beautiful sisters, Sarah and Emily, who are also my best friends for life. The saying "There is no closer friend than a sister" really does ring true in our lives. The two of you have certainly been my biggest cheerleaders! You guys make me brave as I watch the awesome plan of God unfold in your lives.

My parents, who have molded me into the person I am today. Your prayers, spiritual leading, and guidance over the years have paved the way for the three of us girls to be able to run the race that God has intended for us. Thank you from the bottom of my heart for everything you have done for us. Whether it was something big or small, everything made a difference. I couldn't be more thankful for such godly influences in my life, and I'm thankful God entrusted me to the two of you!

My Aunt Lorrie, who is one of my greatest role models in life! You are the ultimate homemaker and woman of God in my eyes, and I aspire to be like you in every way! Thank you for shining Jesus to me and to the world.

Everyone who supports and reads Dashing Dish. You are the heart behind this ministry! Your testimonies and stories affirm the goodness of our faithful God. You bring His message of freedom and hope to life.

Blythe Daniel. Thank you for reaching out and taking me under your wing. You encouraged me every step of the way to keep reaching for the great things God had in store. Thank you for everything you have done to pave the way for me!

Thomas Nelson Publishers, who has made the dream of my first cookbook and devotional book possible. I am so thankful and honored for the opportunity to be working with such a wonderful team of people!

ABOUT THE AUTHOR

Katie Farrell is the creator of Dashing Dish, a healthy recipe website and ministry to women with over 3 million unique visitors a month and more than 14,000 paid monthly subscribers. Katie is a registered nurse from Michigan, where she lives in Brighton with her husband of five years. Dashing Dish is a combination of Katie's passions—helping women find their identity in God and ending misconceptions about healthy eating. Katie wants to inspire women to find the balance between spiritual and physical health, all while enjoying the journey! She has been featured in *Shape*, *Woman's Day*, *O*, *Huffington Post*, and *Foodgawker* and is a featured contributor for Fox News and Roo Mag.

INDEX